ALGEBRA-I EOC TEST PREP

HIGH SCHOOL MATH WORKBOOK

SAVITA MAHESHWARI

Revised Edition, Feb 2023: This edition is redesigned to align more closely to the new changes made in STAAR 2022-23, with a variety of new question types in addition to traditional multiple-choice questions. The new questions are designed to help students transition to the new online STAAR exam.

Revised Edition, Dec 2022: This edition has more than 500 highest quality Algebra 1 EOC Exam based problems across all 7 sections including **70+ solved problems** to sharpen your Algebra skills. You'll find everything you need to build confidence, skills, and knowledge for the highest score possible in Algebra I.

Revised Edition 2021: 2020 was been an unprecedented year for all of us. The world as we knew it, got disrupted, uprooted and handed back upside down. Yet, all of us have marched on bravely in face of this adversity and created our own measures to deal with the aftermath of the pandemic.

Education has probably been impacted the most - with parents, students and teachers all trying to grapple with the best way to maintain continuity in our learning process. Keeping this in mind, the 2021 edition of this book has been reviewed and analyzed to ensure that it meets the needs of any changes that might have come into the learning process. We've ensured the relevance, timeliness and quality of all the contents so that you may find that at least one thing has remain unchanged - the quality that our students expect from us.

Copyright by Smart Math Tutoring.

All rights reserved. This book or any portion thereof may not be reproduced or used in any manner whatsoever without the express written permission of the Smart Math Tutoring

Preface

This practice workbook contains a comprehensive review of the Algebra-I EOC Exam. The questions in this book are styled for standardized Algebra-I end of course exam. With regular practice in solving these questions, the student will feel more confident and better equipped to tackle challenging problems.

About the Author

Savita Maheshwari

Founder of Smart Math Tutoring in Plano, Texas, Savita Maheshwari, is an educator with 15+ years of experience. She has also held the position of an Associate College Professor in a reputed engineering college in India. An Electronics & Communications Engineer turned math teacher; she has a proven record of instilling in her students' a deep love for the subject along with improving their performance on the grade sheet. Her passion and rich experience in teaching are reflected in her classroom and course material. She believes in developing a valuable mental ability, making Math more interesting for students, and improving their conceptual and thinking skills. Because of her talent and commitment, she has received love and respect from a large community of students and their parents. Now, she has distilled her years of experience into a series of publications making sure it holds the best content a student can find to improve their math skills.

Complimentary Counseling Session

Dear Teachers & Students,

We thank you for taking a firm step towards improving your Mathematical abilities. The book you have just purchased has been built with hours of dedication and is trusted by thousands of students like you. Yet, we understand that no two students are identical and each one needs personalized attention.

As a token of our appreciation for your support, **we would like to offer you a free 30-minute counseling session with the author - Savita Maheshwari**. This session is designed to help you understand how to effectively use this workbook and improve your test score. Please reach out to **info@smartmathtutoring.com** to schedule your free session (Mention subject as "Complimentary Counseling Session").

We always welcome any feedback, suggestions, or queries through email to info@smartmathtutoring.com.

With Best Wishes

Smart Math Tutoring

Contents

Complimentary Counseling Session with Author
Reference Sheet

1. Linear equations and inequality..1
2. Answer Key - Linear equations and inequality 35
3. Relations, Functions and Arithmetic sequence..37
4. Answer Key - Relations, Functions and Arithmetic sequence 65
5. Different Forms of Linear equations..67
6. Answer Key - Different Forms of Linear equations 117
7. System of Linear equations and Inequality..119
8. Answer Key - System of Linear equations and Inequality 145
9. Radicals, Exponents and Exponential functions...147
10. Answer Key - Radicals, Exponents and Exponential functions 175
11. Polynomial Functions..177
12. Answer Key - Polynomial Functions 199
13. Quadratic Functions..201
14. Answer Key - Quadratic Functions 229
15. Solutions – Linear equations and inequality..231
16. Solutions – Relations, Functions and Arithmetic sequence......................233
17. Solutions – Different Forms of Linear equations.......................................235
18. Solutions – System of Linear equations and Inequality............................237
19. Solutions – Radicals, Exponents and Exponential functions....................239
20. Solutions – Polynomial Functions..241
21. Solutions – Quadratic Functions..243

Reference Material

FACTORING

Perfect square trinomials	$a^2 + 2ab + b^2 = (a + b)^2$ $a^2 - 2ab + b^2 = (a - b)^2$
Difference of squares	$a^2 - b^2 = (a - b)(a + b)$

PROPERTIES OF EXPONENTS

Product of powers	$a^m a^n = a^{(m+n)}$
Quotient of powers	$\dfrac{a^m}{a^n} = a^{(m-n)}$
Power of a power	$(a^m)^n = a^{mn}$
Rational exponent	$a^{\frac{m}{n}} = \sqrt[n]{a^m}$
Negative exponent	$a^{-n} = \dfrac{1}{a^n}$

LINEAR EQUATIONS

Standard form	$Ax + By = C$
Slope-intercept form	$y = mx + b$
Point-slope form	$y - y_1 = m(x - x_1)$
Slope of a line	$m = \dfrac{y_2 - y_1}{x_2 - x_1}$

QUADRATIC EQUATIONS

Standard form	$f(x) = ax^2 + bx + c$
Vertex form	$f(x) = a(x - h)^2 + k$
Quadratic formula	$x = \dfrac{-b \pm \sqrt{b^2 - 4ac}}{2a}$
Axis of symmetry	$x = \dfrac{-b}{2a}$

CHAPTER 1

LINEAR EQUATION AND INEQUALITIES

LINEAR EQUATION AND INEQUALITIES

1. Ms. Carol spends $75 each month eating out at fast food restaurants. She plans to reduce her spending for fast food by $5 each month until she has reduced her spending to $25 per month. Which equation can be used to determine m, the number of months it will take for Ms. Carol to reduce her fast-food spending to $25 per month?

   A. $\frac{1}{3}(5m + 75) = 25$
   B. $75 - 5m = 25$
   C. $5m + 75m = 25$
   D. $\frac{1}{3}m + 75 = 25$

2. The sum of negative twenty-nine and twenty-eight is negative seven more than a number. What is the number? Record your answer in the space provided below.

3. Mrs. Mandela is buying folding table that are on sale for $25. If she has $85, which inequality can be solved to show the number of tables 't' can she buy?

   A. 25t ≤ 85
   B. 25t ≥ 85
   C. 25t > 85
   D. 25t < 85

LINEAR EQUATION AND INEQUALITIES

4. Frost is helping the manager of the local produce market to expand her business by distributing flyers around the neighborhood. He gets paid $15 a day as well as $0.10 for every flyer he distributes. Frost would like to earn at least $85 each day. Which of the following represents this situation, where x is the number of flyers distributed?
   A. $15 + 0.10x \leq 85$
   B. $15 + x \leq 85$
   C. $15 + 0.10x \geq 85$
   D. $15 + x \geq 85$

5. Jonathan is considering accepting one of two sales positions. MNC Company offers a yearly salary of $48,000. PQR Company offers a yearly salary of $41,000 plus a 2% annual commission on sales. For what amount of sales 's' is the salary at PQR Company greater than the salary at MNC Company?
   A. $s > 8000$
   B. $s > 35,000$
   C. $s > 80,000$
   D. $s > 350,000$

6. Solve $\dfrac{4}{s} = \dfrac{-2}{9}$.

   Solve for 's' and record your answer in the space provided below.

LINEAR EQUATION AND INEQUALITIES

7. Solve $m - 9 \leq 17$.
   A. $m \leq 8$
   B. $m \geq 8$
   C. $m \leq 26$
   D. $m \geq 26$

8. Rhea scored *p* points in the first half of the basketball game. In the second half, she scored 5 more than $\frac{1}{4}$ of the number of points she scored in the first half of the game. Altogether, she scored 25 points in the game. The following equation represents this situation where *p* represents the number of points Rhea scored in the first half.

   $$p + \left(\frac{1}{4}p + 5\right) = 25$$

   How many points did Rhea score in the first half?
   A. 16
   B. 19
   C. 12
   D. 18

9. A manufacturing company is building a rectangular room in their warehouse to store their products. The length of the room is 1 more than 4 times its width. The perimeter of the room is 62 meters. Select the choices which represent the length 'l' in terms of width 'w' and Perimeter in terms of 'l' and 'w'?

A. l = w+4	C. w+(w+4) = 62
B. l = 4w+1	D. (4w+1)+w =62
	E. w+(w+4) = 31
	F. (4w+1)+w =31

LINEAR EQUATION AND INEQUALITIES

10. Which of the following is the solution to this inequality?

    $3(5 + 2n) \geq 7 + 10n$

    A. $n \geq 2$

    B. $n \geq -2$

    C. $n \leq 2$

    D. $n \leq -2$

11. Employees at the bakery factory are packing cartons of bread. One carton can hold x breads. Today the employees have B bread to pack. When they have finished, they have packed C cartons and have 4 breads left over. Use the equation $\frac{B}{x} = C + \frac{4}{x}$ to find C, the number of cartons that were packed.

    A. $C = \frac{B-4}{x}$

    B. $C = \frac{B}{x} - 4$

    C. $C = \frac{B}{x-4}$

    D. $C = 4 - \frac{B}{x}$

12. $\frac{5a}{7} - 21 = -46$; solve for a.

    A. -32

    B. $-83\frac{2}{5}$

    C. -55

    D. -35

LINEAR EQUATION AND INEQUALITIES

13. Which statements shows the solution set of the compound inequality?
    $8x - 21 < 2x$ and $3x + 5 \geq -1$?

    A. $x \leq -2$
    B. $x \geq -2$
    C. $x < -2$
    D. $x > 3.5$
    E. $x < 3.5$

14. Which graph shows the solution set of the compound inequality
    $4(3x - 5) > 4(2x - 7)$ or $2x - 10 < 4x$.

    A. 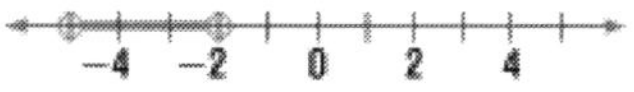 ![number line -4 to 4]
    B. 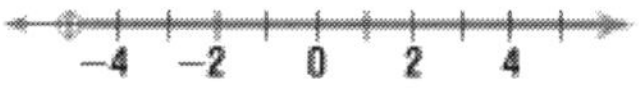 ![number line -4 to 4]
    C. 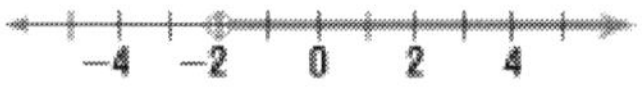 ![number line -4 to 4]
    D. 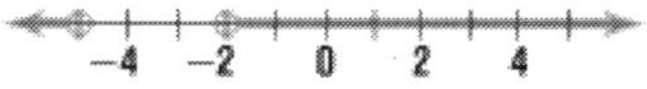 ![number line -4 to 4]

15. Which of the following graphs represents this linear equation?

$$y = -2x - 5$$

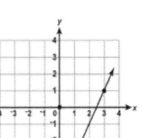

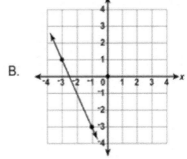
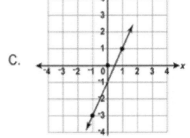
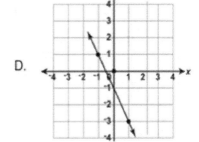

16. Solve -18b > -198.
    A. b > 11
    B. b < 3,564
    C. b > 3,564
    D. b < 11

17. Solve −4(10 − n) − 6n > 8(n + 3) − 7n + 2.
    A. n < -6
    B. n > -22
    C. n > -6
    D. n < -22

LINEAR EQUATION AND INEQUALITIES

18. Choose the graph of the solution to the inequality $4(x + 3) < 3x + 10$.

   A. [number line with closed circle at -2, shaded left]
   B. [number line with open circle at -2, shaded left]
   C. [number line with open circle at -2, shaded right]
   D. [number line with open circle at 2, shaded left]

19. Choose the inequality that corresponds with the sentence "Twice a number increased by four is less than the difference of three times that number and five."

   A. $2x + 4 < 5 - 3x$
   B. $2x + 4 > 3x - 5$
   C. $2x + 4 < 3x - 5$
   D. $2(x + 4) < 3(x - 5)$

20. Solve $-15k > 135$.

   A. $k > 9$
   B. $k < 9$
   C. $k > -9$
   D. $k < -9$

21. Solve $-6x - 12 > -18$. Select the correct answer for each box.

   x [A. < B. >]   [C. 1 D. -1 E. 5 F. -5]

LINEAR EQUATION AND INEQUALITIES

22. $5x - 5 = 5x - 9$
    A. −4
    B. No solution
    C. Infinite solution
    D. −3

23. Sameera earns 1.5 times her normal hourly pay for each hour that she works over 35 hours in a week. Her normal pay is p dollars per hour. Last week Sameera worked 51 hours and earned $515.75. Which equation represents this situation?
    A. 35p + 1.5p = 515.75
    B. 35p + 16(1.5p) = 515.75
    C. 35 + 51(1.5p) = 515.75
    D. None of the above

24. Which situation does not show causation?
    A. More exercise burns more calories.
    B. Number of firemen fighting fire increases as size of fire increases.
    C. Windmill spin faster because of stronger winds.
    D. Finding more mess in 3rd period than 1st period in a class.

LINEAR EQUATION AND INEQUALITIES

25. Natalie is driving 192 miles to Alaska for a math convention. She has already driven x miles of the trip. If Natalie drives below 60 miles per hour for the remainder of the trip, which inequality best represents the amount of time in hours, t, that it will take her to complete the remainder of her drive to Alaska?

   A. $t < \frac{192-x}{60}$
   B. $t > \frac{60}{192-x}$
   C. $t < \frac{60}{192-x}$
   D. $t > \frac{192-x}{60}$

26. Ginnie and her cousin went to a restaurant for dinner. Ginnie dinner cost $15 more than her cousin's. If their combined bill was under $65, which inequality best describes the cost of their dinners?

   A. $x + 15 < 65x$
   B. $x + (x + 15) < 65$
   C. $x + (x + 65) < 15$
   D. $x - (x + 15) < 65$

27. Doremon Mobile Service Station uses the graph below to determine how much a mechanic should charge for labor for automobile repairs.

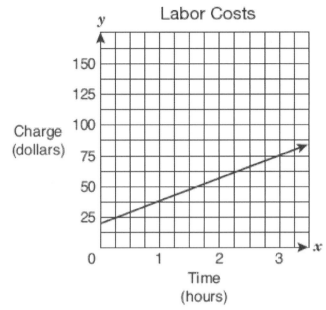

Labor Costs

If the labor charge on an automobile repair bill was $67.50, for approximately how many hours, h, did the mechanic work?

A. $2.25 < h < 2.50$
B. $2.75 < h < 3.00$
C. $2.00 < h < 2.25$
D. $2.50 < h < 2.75$

28. A student incorrectly solved the equation $3(2x + 6) - 4 = 14$ as shown below.

    Step 1: $6x + 6 - 4 = 14$

    Step 2: $6x + 2 = 14$

    Step 3: $6x = 12$

    Step 4: $x = 2$

    In what step did the student first make a mistake?

    A. In Step 1, the student should have multiplied both terms in parentheses by 3, not just the first term.

    B. In Step 2, the student should have subtracted 4 from the right side of the equation, not the left side.

    C. In Step 3, the student should have added 2 to both sides of the equation instead of subtracting 2.

    D. In Step 4, the student should have multiplied both sides of the equation by 6 instead of dividing by 6.

29. Is the equation $4(2x-8) = -18$ equivalent to $8x-32 = -18$?

    A. Yes, the equations are equivalent by the Associative Property of Multiplication

    B. Yes, the equations are equivalent by the Commutative Property of Multiplication

    C. Yes, the equations are equivalent by the Distributive Property of Multiplication over Addition

    D. No, the equations are not equivalent

LINEAR EQUATION AND INEQUALITIES

30. The Palio Pizza restaurant has used the following equation to calculate the number of Pizza trays needed for a very large party.
    Which equation is equivalent to 4(3 +5x) = 6 − 2(1 − 4x).
    A. 8x = -24
    B. 6x = 15
    C. 12x = -8
    D. 28x = 17

31. Kiara's solution to an equation is shown below.
    Given: $n + 8(n + 20) = 110$
    Step 1: $n + 8n + 20 = 110$
    Step 2: $9n + 20 = 110$
    Step 3: $9n = 110 - 20$
    Step 4: $9n = 90$
    Step 5: $\frac{9n}{9} = \frac{90}{9}$
    Step 6: $n = 10$
    Which statement about Kiara's solution is true?
    A. Kiara's solution is correct.
    B. Kiara made a mistake in Step 1.
    C. Kiara made a mistake in Step 3.
    D. Kiara made a mistake in Step 5.

32. What is the solution to the inequality below?
    $2x - 7 \geq 17$
    A. $x \leq 12$
    B. $x \geq 12$
    C. $x \leq 5$
    D. $x \geq 5$

33. Which graph represents the solution set for $\frac{1}{2} - \frac{2}{3}x < \frac{5}{6}$?

A.

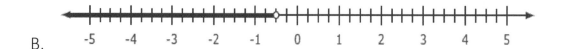
B.

C.

D.

34. Which inequality is shown by the graph below?

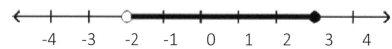

A. $-2 \leq w \leq 3$
B. $-2 < w \leq 3$
C. $w \geq 3$ and $w < -2$
D. $-2 > w \geq 3$

35. Which of the following is the solution to the inequality?
$x + 6 > 4(x + 3)$
A. $x < -2$
B. $x > 2$
C. $x > -1.6$
D. $x < -1.6$

LINEAR EQUATION AND INEQUALITIES

36. A bakery has an order to make 150 cupcakes. The workers can frost and decorate 4 cupcakes per minute. Let x be the number of minutes the workers have been working. Write an inequality that says the number of cupcakes remaining to be decorated is less than 20.
    A. $4x - 150 < 20$
    B. $150 + 4x < 20$
    C. $150 - 4x \leq 20$
    D. $150 - 4x < 20$

37. A student is ordering a flower arrangement. She can choose any combination of tulip and carnations for her flower arrangement, and she does not want to spend more than $45.
    If tulip cost $5 each and carnations cost $3 each, which inequality represents all possible combinations of x tulips and y carnations?

A	B	C	D	E	F	G	H
>	≥	<	≤	3	5	15	45

    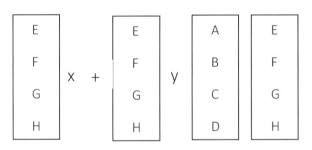

38. Which ordered pair is in the solution set of $y \geq \frac{1}{3}x + 4$?
    A. $(-6, 1)$
    B. $(-1, 6)$
    C. $(6, -1)$
    D. $(1, -6)$

39. Which statements are NOT true for the given data in the table?

x	1	2	3	4	5
y	-3	-2	-1	0	1

A. It is a linear function.
B. It is not a linear function.
C. Y-intercept of the given function is 4.
D. X-intercept of the function is 4.
E. Point (22,18) belongs to the given function.

40. The temperature of air in a room that began at 55°F is increasing by 8°F per hour. The following equation represents this situation:

$$y = 55 + 8x$$

Where x represents the number of hours and y represents the temperature.

Which of the following is a graph of this equation?

A.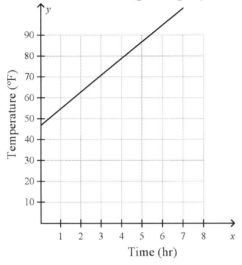

C.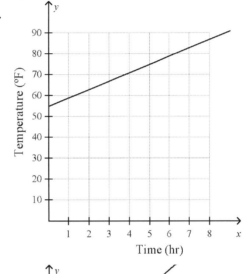

B.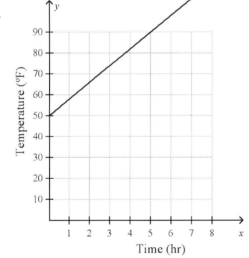

D.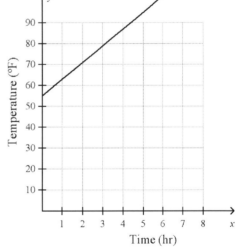

LINEAR EQUATION AND INEQUALITIES

41. Translate "two times a number is six times the sum of z and y" into an equation.
    A. $2x = 6(zy)$
    B. $2 + x = 6 + z + y$
    C. $2x = 6(z + y)$
    D. $2x = 6z + y$

42. Translate $3x + 5y = 7$ into a verbal sentence.
    A. The sum of 3 times x- and 5-times y is 7.
    B. The sum of 3 and x plus the product of 5 and y is 7.
    C. x to the third power plus y to the fifth power is 7.
    D. 3 times the sum of x and y is 7.

43. Write an equation for the following word problem.
    A number is 7 times another number. The sum of these two numbers is 64.
    A. $y + y = 64$
    B. $y = 64$
    C. $y = 7(64)$
    D. $y + 7y = 64$

LINEAR EQUATION AND INEQUALITIES

44. A pair of footwear costs $62.33 and the state sales tax is 8%. Use the formula $C = p + rp$ to find the total cost of the footwear, where C is the total cost, p is the price, and r is the sales tax rate.
    A. $95.38
    B. $60.99
    C. $67.31
    D. $78.19

45. Evaluate $|-x - 2y|$ for $x = -12$ and $y = 8$.
    A. 4
    B. 8
    C. −4
    D. −8

LINEAR EQUATION AND INEQUALITIES

46. Guy keeps track of the amount of water he uses on his flower garden over the course of the summer. He finds that the less it rains, the more he needs to water the garden to keep his plants healthy and in bloom. This summer the two driest months were June and August, but it rained so heavily in September that he did not have to water his garden at all during that month. Which of the following graphs best represents Guy's water usage this summer?

A.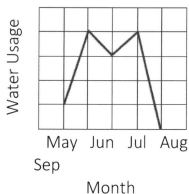

B.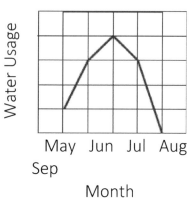

C.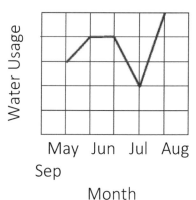

D.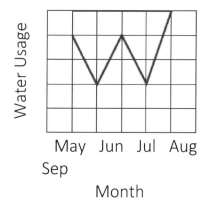

LINEAR EQUATION AND INEQUALITIES

47. To which of the following situations can the function y = 9x + 15 best be applied?
    A. The number of miles a person walks if he walks for 9 hours at the rate of 15 miles per hour
    B. The total weight on a scale if 9 pounds is placed there initially and a series of 15-pound weights are added to it
    C. The total wages earned by a waiter who is paid $9 per hour and earns $15 in tips
    D. The combined length of 9 boards, each 15 feet longer than the width of a doorway

48. The population of Williston is currently 21,200 people. If the population increases at an average rate of 415 people per year, which equation could be used to find the approximate number of years it will take for the population to reach 27000 people?
    A. $21,200 + 415n = 27000$
    B. $415n = 27000$
    C. $21,200n + 415 = 27000$
    D. $21,200n = 27000$

49. Which equation represents the data in the table?

x	0	1	2	3	4
y	-4	-2	0	2	4

    A. $y = x - 4$
    B. $y = 2x - 2$
    C. $y = 2x - 4$
    D. $y = 4x - 4$

LINEAR EQUATION AND INEQUALITIES

50. The values in the table show a linear relationship. Find the slope.

x	6	8	11	15
y	4	10	19	31

A. 3
B. -3
C. $\frac{1}{3}$
D. $-\frac{1}{3}$

51. Venus joins a fitness club that has a membership fee of $40 plus $25 per month. Saturn's club has a fee of $60 and charges $20 per month. In how many months will the two clubs cost the same? Record your answer in the space provided below.

52. You've saved $260 and plan to spend $21 for each music CD you purchase. Write an equation to represent d, the amount of dollars remaining, as a function of c, the number of CDs you purchase.

A. $c = 21d$
B. $d = 21c$
C. $c = 21d - 260$
D. $d = 260 - 21c$

53. A decorator charge $35 for an initial consultation, then $65 per hour. Another decorator just charges $100 per hour. How long is a job for which the two decorators charge the same price?

    A. 1 hour
    B. 2 hours
    C. 4 hours
    D. 8 hours

54. The scatter plot shows the relationship between the weekly total sales ($) and the number of different minutes of TV advertising the store purchased. Based on this relationship, use the line of best fit to predict what the total sales will be when the store has paid for 150 minutes of advertising.

    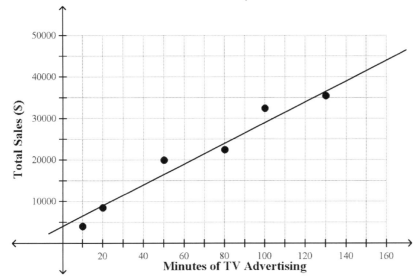

    A. $35,000
    B. $38,000
    C. $40,000
    D. $42,000

LINEAR EQUATION AND INEQUALITIES

55. Simon is on page 60 of her book and reads 6 pages every night. Jonas is on page 70 of the same book and reads 5 pages every night. How long will it take Simon to be further in the book than Jonas?
    A. 3 nights
    B. 11 nights
    C. 15 nights
    D. 10 nights

56. Find the constant of proportionality from the table below.

X	2	5	7	9
Y	0.4	1	1.4	1.8

    A. 0.6
    B. 2
    C. 5
    D. 0.2

57. Which of the following tables show proportion relationship? Select more than ONE answer.

    A.
x	y
1	-3
2	-6
3	-9
4	-12
5	-15

    B.
x	y
-4	-8
-2	-4
0	0
2	4
4	8

    C.
x	y
-1	-6
0	-5
1	-3
2	0
3	4

    D.
x	y
-1	-1.5
1	1.5
3	4.5
5	7.5
7	10.5

LINEAR EQUATION AND INEQUALITIES

58. Write an equation of the direct variation that includes the point (12, −15). Record your answer in the space provided below.

   [   ]

59. Find the constant of variation k for the proportional equation. Then find an equation for the given values. Select ONE answer from each box.

   $y = 4.5$ when $x = 3$

   Constant of variation is
   - $\frac{3}{2}$
   - $\frac{2}{3}$
   - 3

   and equation is given by
   - $y = \frac{3x}{2}$
   - $y = \frac{3}{2x}$
   - $y = 3x$
   - $y = \frac{2x}{3}$

60. Find the constant of proportionality from the equations below:
   $$0.5y = 7.25x$$

61. Which graph shows proportional relation?

A.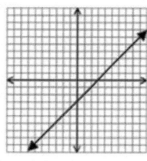

B.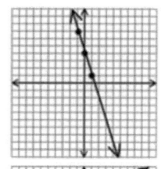

C.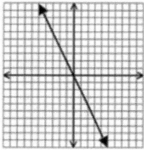

D.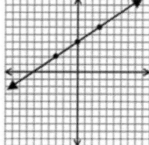

62. $S = \pi r^2 + 2\pi rh$. Solve for h

A. $h = \frac{S + \pi r^2}{2\pi r}$

B. $h = \frac{S - \pi r^2}{2\pi r}$

C. $h = \frac{S + 2\pi r}{\pi r^2}$

D. $h = \frac{S - 2\pi r}{\pi r^2}$

63. $x = \frac{y}{N} + 1$ Solve for N

   A. $N = \frac{x}{y+1}$

   B. $N = \frac{y}{x-1}$

   C. $N = \frac{y}{x+1}$

   D. $N = \frac{x}{y-1}$

64. $\frac{a}{c} = \frac{b}{d}$ Solve for c

   A. $c = \frac{ad}{b}$

   B. $c = \frac{ab}{d}$

   C. $c = \frac{d}{ab}$

   D. $c = \frac{db}{a}$

65. $\frac{1}{a} + \frac{1}{b} = c$ Solve for a

   A. $a = \frac{b}{bc+1}$

   B. $a = \frac{c}{bc-1}$

   C. $a = \frac{b}{bc-1}$

   D. $a = \frac{c}{bc+1}$

LINEAR EQUATION AND INEQUALITIES

66. $C = \frac{5}{9}(F - 32)$ Solve for F

   A. $F = \frac{5C}{9} + 32$

   B. $F = \frac{9C}{5} + 32$

   C. $F = \frac{5C}{9} - 32$

   D. $F = \frac{9C}{5} - 32$

67. $F = \frac{mv^2}{r}$ Solve for m

   A. $m = \frac{Fv^2}{r}$

   B. $m = \frac{Fr^2}{v}$

   C. $m = \frac{Fr}{v^2}$

   D. $m = \frac{rv^2}{F}$

68. Find the constant of variation k for the direct variation.

x	F(x)
-1	3
0	0
2	-6
5	-15

   A. k = 3

   B. k = –0.33

   C. k = –3

   D. k = 0.33

LINEAR EQUATION AND INEQUALITIES

69. Write an equation of the direct variation that includes the point (9, −12).

    A. $y = 1\frac{1}{3}x$

    B. $y = \frac{1}{12}x$

    C. $y = -1\frac{1}{3}x$

    D. $y = -\frac{3}{4}x$

70. Select functions which are not examples of direct variation?

    A. $x - 6y = 0$

    B. $2x - 5y = 3$

    C. $Y = 0.8x + 1$

    D. $5x = y$

    E. $Y = x^2$

    F. $Y = x - 1$

71. Use the direct variation equation $y = 88x$ to find x when $y = 22$.

    A. $x = 1936$

    B. $x = -4$

    C. $x = 4$

    D. $x = \frac{1}{4}$

LINEAR EQUATION AND INEQUALITIES

72. Ryan is writing a composition for homework. He decides to keep track of the number of sentences he writes compared to the time in minutes he works. The graph below shows the data he collected.

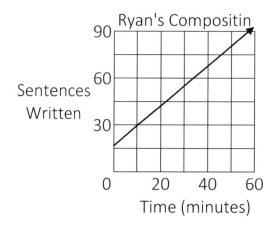

At what rate does Ryan write his composition?
A. 0.5 sentence per minute
B. 1 sentence per minute
C. 1.5 sentences per minute
D. 2 sentences per minute

73. A North Alabama farmer knows that the number of potatoes harvested varies directly with the number of potato plants grown. Last year the farmer harvested 342 potatoes from 9 potato plants. If the farmer plants 14 potato plants this year, how many potatoes can he expect to harvest?
A. 532
B. 523
C. 294
D. 2646

LINEAR EQUATION AND INEQUALITIES

74. The data in the table show the cost of renting a bicycle by the hour, including a deposit.

    Renting a Bicycle

Hours (h)	Cost in dollars (c)
2	17
5	32
8	47

    If hours, h, were graphed on the horizontal axis, and cost, c, were graphed on the vertical axis, what would be the equation of a line that fits the data?
    A. $c = 5h + 5$
    B. $c = \frac{1}{5}h + 7$
    C. $c = 5h + 7$
    D. $c = 5h - 5$

75. Shanky is constructing an isosceles triangle to use as a model in her Algebra class. The perimeter of her triangle is 27 inches. Shanky uses the equation $b = 27 - 2s$ to find b, the length of the triangle's third side, in terms of s, the length of each of its two congruent sides. What is her equation written in terms of s?
    A. $s = 2(b + 27)$
    B. $s = \frac{27+b}{2}$
    C. $s = 2(b - 27)$
    D. $s = \frac{27-b}{2}$

LINEAR EQUATION AND INEQUALITIES

76. The pressure exerted on the floor by a person's shoe heel depends on the weight of the person and the width of the heel. The formula is
$$P = \frac{2.6w}{H^2},$$
where P is pressure in pounds per square inch, W is weight in pounds, and H is heel width in inches. Which of the following shows the pressure formula solved for H?

A. $H = \pm\sqrt{2.6WP}$

B. $H = \pm\sqrt{\frac{2.6W}{P}}$

C. $H = \pm\frac{2.6W}{P}$

D. $H = \frac{2.6W}{2P}$

77. Students in grades 6, 7, and 8 sold a total of 540 concert tickets. Grade 6 students sold x tickets. Grade 7 students sold y tickets and Grade 8 students sold t tickets.

Use the equation $x + y + t = 540$ to find x, the number of tickets that were sold by Grade 6 students.

A. $x = 320 - t + y$

B. $x = 540 - t - y$

C. $x = 540 + t - y$

D. $x = y - t - 540$

LINEAR EQUATION AND INEQUALITIES

78. A video store charges a monthly membership fee of $7.50, but the charge to rent each movie is only $1.00 per movie. Another store has no membership fee, but it cost $2.50 to rent each movie. The equation below represents this situation where *m* is the number of movies rented each month.

$$7.50 + 1.00m = 2.50m$$

Which of the following is the number of movies that need to be rented each month for the total fees to be same from either store?

A. 3 movies
B. 5 movies
C. 7 movies
D. 9 movies

79. Isabel reads 12 books from the library each month for *m* months in a row. Each month her sister, Emma, reads $\frac{1}{2}$ as many books as Isabel reads. Together they have read 108 books. The following equation represents this situation where *m* is the number of months that the girls have read.

$$12m + \frac{1}{2}(12m) = 108$$

Which of the following is the number of months it took Isabel and Emma to read 108 books? Record your answer in the space provided below.

80. Solve $y + w - \frac{4}{5}z = 0$ for z.

   A. $z = \frac{5}{4}(y + w)$

   B. $z = \frac{4}{5}(y + w)$

   C. $z = \frac{5}{4}w + y$

   D. $z = \frac{5y}{4} + w$

Answer Key – Linear equation and Inequalities

		Marks (C/W)			Marks (C/W)			Marks (C/W)
1	B		31	B		61	C	
2	6		32	B		62	B	
3	A		33	A		63	B	
4	C		34	B		64	A	
5	D		35	A		65	C	
6	-18		36	D		66	B	
7	C		37	F, E, D, H		67	C	
8	A		38	B		68	C	
9	B, F		39	B, C		69	C	
10	C		40	D		70	B, C, E, F	
11	A		41	C		71	D	
12	D		42	A		72	C	
13	B, E		43	D		73	A	
14	B		44	C		74	C	
15	B		45	A		75	D	
16	D		46	A		76	B	
17	D		47	C		77	B	
18	B		48	A		78	B	
19	C		49	C		79	6	
20	D		50	A		80	A	
21	A, C		51	4 Months				
22	B		52	D				
23	B		53	A				
24	D		54	D				
25	D		55	B				
26	B		56	D				
27	D		57	A, B, D				
28	A		58	4y+5x =0				
29	C		59	$\frac{3}{2}$, $y=\frac{3x}{2}$				
30	C		60	14.5				
	Total			Total			Total	

SECTION 2

RELATIONS, FUNCTIONS AND ARITHMATIC SEQUENCE

RELATIONS, FUNCTIONS & ARITHMATIC SEQUENCE

1. Identify the mapping diagram that represents the relation and determine whether this relation is a function.

   {(−8, −6), (−5, 2), (−8,1), (7,3)}

   a.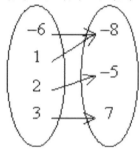

   The relation is a function.

   c.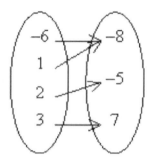

   The relation is not a function

   b.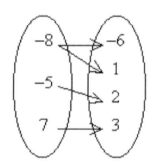

   The relation is a function.

   d.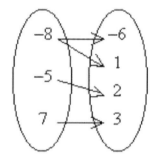

   The relation is not a function.

2. Give the domain and range of the relation.

x	y
3	7
6	13
0	0
−7	−13

   A. D: {3, 6, −7, 7, 13, −13}; R: {0}
   B. D: {−7, 0, 3, 6}; R: {−13, 0, 7, 13}
   C. D: all real numbers; R: all real numbers
   D. D: {−13, 0, 7, 13}; R: {−7, 0, 3, 6}

RELATIONS, FUNCTIONS & ARITHMATIC SEQUENCE

3. Which of the following relations is a function?
   A. $\{(-2,-2),(-2,-1),(-2,0),(-2,1),(-2,2)\}$
   B. $\{(1,0),(-1,0),(2,1)(-2,1)(3,2)(-3,2)\}$
   C. $\{(-2,1),(-1,2),(0,0),(-1,1),(2,-2)\}$
   D. $\{(-3,3),(1,3)(-3,2)(1,2)(-3,1)(1,1)\}$

4. Find g(-4) if $g(x) = 3x^3 - 1$.

5. A new school has opened. Students are allowed into the school at 8:00 Am. Classes start at 9:00 AM. Students must leave the building by 5:00 PM. The pop machine is filled twice a day, once at 7:00 AM. Answer the questions listed using the graph below.

   Number of cans vs. Time of day

   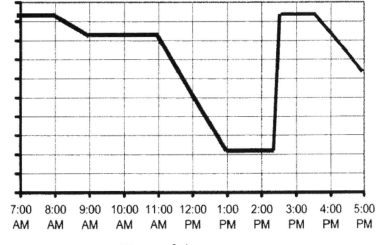

   At what time did the pop machine get refilled?
   A. 2:00 pm
   B. 11:00 am
   C. 2:30 pm
   D. 1:00 pm

RELATIONS, FUNCTIONS & ARITHMATIC SEQUENCE

6. Write a function rule for the table.

Hour Worked 'h'	Pay 'p'
2	$15.00
4	$30.00
6	$45.00
8	$60.00

A. $p = 7.50h$

B. $p = 15h$

C. $p = h + 15$

D. $h = 7.50p$

7. Evaluate $f(x) = -3x - 7$ for $x = 3$.

A. −11

B. 1

C. −16

D. 11

8. Write a function rule for the table.

x	f(x)
3	7
4	8
5	9
6	10

A. $f(x) = x - 4$

B. $f(x) = 4x$

C. $f(x) = x + 4$

D. $f(x) = -4 - x$

RELATIONS, FUNCTIONS & ARITHMATIC SEQUENCE

9. Write a function rule that gives the total cost $c(p)$ of p pounds of sugar if each pound costs $0.59.

   A. $c(p) = 59p$
   B. $c(p) = \dfrac{p}{0.59}$
   C. $c(p) = p + 0.59$
   D. $c(p) = 0.59p$

10. Which of the following relation shown below represent y as a function of x? Select ONE correct answer in each row.

Relation	Function	Not a Function
Y = 4x	A	B
Y = x - 3	A	B
X = 5	A	B
(graph)	A	B
(graph)	A	B
x: 1, 2, 5, 6 / y: 4, 4, 5, 4	A	B

RELATIONS, FUNCTIONS & ARITHMATIC SEQUENCE

11. Which of the following equations describes the same function in the table below?

x	y
2	8
3	13
4	18
5	23

A. $y = 5x - 2$
B. $y = \frac{1}{5}x - 2$
C. $y = 5x + 2$
D. $y = \frac{1}{5}x + 2$

12. What is the range of the relation shown in the graph below?

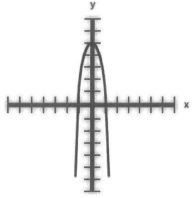

A. $y \leq 5$
B. $x \leq 5$
C. All values of y
D. All values of x

RELATIONS, FUNCTIONS & ARITHMATIC SEQUENCE

13. For f(x) = 24 - 2x, find f (2) and find x such that f(x) = 10.
    A. 28; 12
    B. 22; 4
    C. 20; 7
    D. 22; 7

14. Which graph is the most appropriate to describe a quantity decreasing at a steady rate?

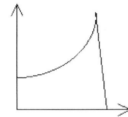
a.

c.

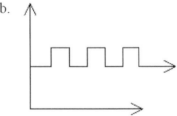
b.

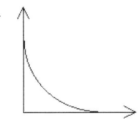
d.

15. For $f(x) = 3x + 4$, find $f(2)$ and find x such that $f(x) = 17$. Select one answers from each box.

$f(2) =$
- A. 9
- B. 10
- C. 12

$x =$
- D. 7
- E. $\frac{13}{3}$
- F. $\frac{10}{3}$

RELATIONS, FUNCTIONS & ARITHMATIC SEQUENCE

16. Select the statements which are TRUE for given function values.

x	y
3	7
10	21
0	0
−2	−3

A. Domain is all real numbers.
B. Given function is discrete.
C. Given function is continuous.
D. Range is {-3, 0, 7, 21}.
E. Given relation is not a function.
F. It is not a linear function.

17. Determine which of the following graphs represent a function.

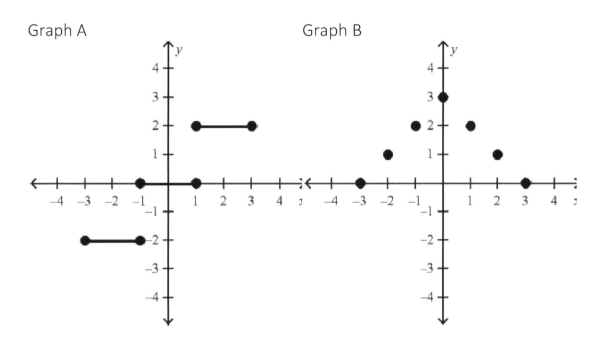

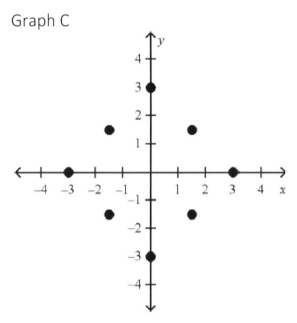

A. None of the graphs are functions.
B. Graph B is a function.
C. Graphs A and B are functions.
D. Graphs B and C are functions.

18. Give the domain and range of the relation. (You can take approximate values of x and y.

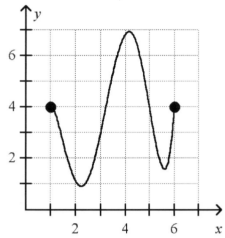

A. D: $0 \leq x \leq 7$; R: $1 \leq y \leq 7$
B. D: $1 \leq x \leq 6$; R: $1 \leq y \leq 7$
C. D: $2 \leq x \leq 6$; R: $4 \leq y \leq 7$
D. D: $1 \leq x \leq 7$; R: $1 \leq y \leq 6$

19. Given $f(x) = 3 - x$ with domain D: $\{-2, -1, 0, 1, 2\}$. What is the range, R?
    A. R: $\{5, 4, 0, 1, 2\}$
    B. R: $\{5, 4, 0, 2, 1\}$
    C. R: $\{1, 2, 3, 4, 5\}$
    D. R: $\{-1, -2, 3, 1, 2\}$

20. Which of the following relations is a function?
    A. {(1, 0), (1, -1), (2, 0), (2, -1), (3, 0), (3, -1)}
    B. {(1, 3), (-1, 5), (2, 7), (-2, 7), (3, 5), (-3, 3)}
    C. {(-2, -1), (1, -2), (0, 0), (-1, -1), (-2, -2)}
    D. {(0, 3), (1, 3), (-3, 3), (1, 2), (-3, 2), (1, 3)}

21. Graph $x + 2y = -2$ for the domain D: $\{-4, -2, 0, 2, 4\}$.

A.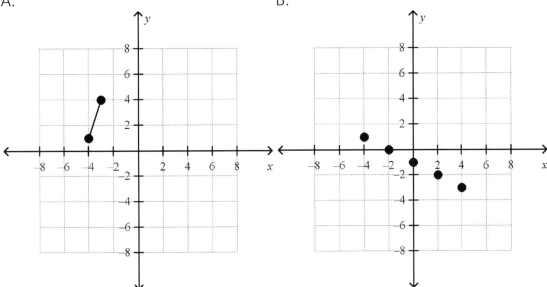
B.

C.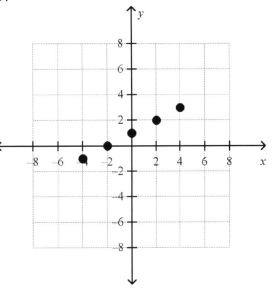
D.

RELATIONS, FUNCTIONS & ARITHMATIC SEQUENCE

22. What are the domain and range of function below? Select the correct answers.

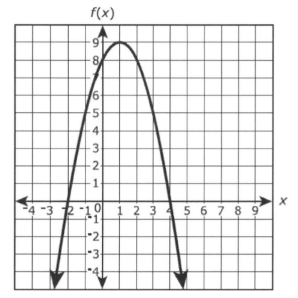

A. Domain: All real numbers

B. Range: All real numbers

C. Domain: $-3 \leq x \leq 5$

D. Range: $y \leq 9$

E. Domain: $-2 \leq x \leq 4$

F. Range: $y \geq -5$

23. The function f is defined by f(x) = -x² and g is defined by $g(x) = -3x + 2$. Which statement is true?

A. $f(-2)$ is greater than $g(-2)$.

B. $f(-2)$ is less than $g(-1)$.

C. $f(0)$ is greater than $g(0)$.

D. $f(1)$ is less than $g(1)$.

24. The function r(x) represents the radius of a circle for a given area x. A graph of the function is shown in the figure.

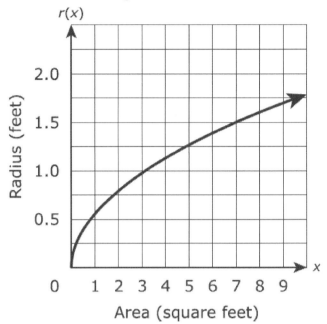

According to the graph what is the approximate average rate of change in the radius of the circle as the area increases from 3 square feet to 7 square feet?

A. 0.125 foot per square foot
B. 0.25 foot per square foot
C. 0.5 foot per square foot
D. 8 feet per square foot

RELATIONS, FUNCTIONS & ARITHMATIC SEQUENCE

25. Give the domain and range of the relation.

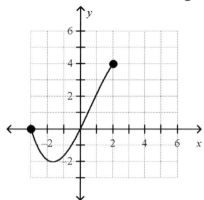

A. D: $-2 \leq x \leq 4$; R: $-3 \leq y \leq 2$
B. D: $-3 \leq x \leq 2$; R: $-2 \leq y \leq 4$
C. D: $-3 \leq x \leq 2$ R: $-3 \leq y \leq 6$
D. D: $-3 \leq x \leq 2$; R: $0 \leq y \leq 4$

26. Given $f(x) = x^2 + 1$ with domain D: {−2, −1,0,1,3} What statements are true?
    A. f(x) is discrete function for given domain.
    B. f(x) is continuous function for given domain.
    C. Range is all real numbers.
    D. Range is {-1, -2, -0, 1, 3}
    E. Range is {1, 2, 5, 10}
    F. Y-intercept of given function is 0.

RELATIONS, FUNCTIONS & ARITHMATIC SEQUENCE

27. Determine which of the following graphs represent a function.

Graph A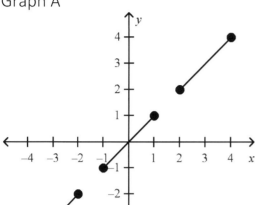

Graph B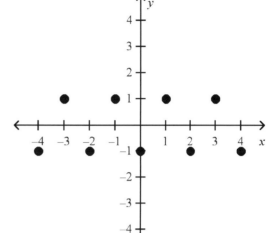

Graph C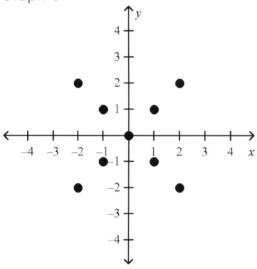

A. None of the graphs are functions.

B. All of the graphs are functions.

C. Graphs A and B are functions.

D. Graphs B and C are functions.

RELATIONS, FUNCTIONS & ARITHMATIC SEQUENCE

28. The graph of part of linear function g is shown on the grid.

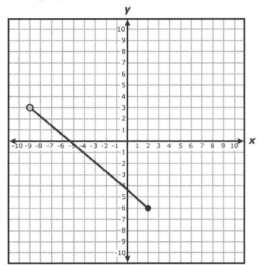

Which inequality best represents the domain of the part shown?

A. $-9 < x \leq 2$

B. $-9 \leq x < 2$

C. $-6 < g(x) \leq 3$

D. $-6 \leq g(x) < 3$

29. If f(x) = -5x + 3, find f(m+2)

A. -5x + 3 + m + 2

B. -5m + 5

C. -5m – 7

D. -5m -13

30. If f(x) = 4x – 2 and f(x) = 18, find x.

A. 74

B. 5

C. 70

D. 20

RELATIONS, FUNCTIONS & ARITHMATIC SEQUENCE

31. If $f(x) = -3x - 8$, For what value of x, $f(x) = 22$? Record your answer in the space provided below.

32.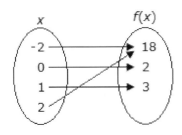

Which function best represents the above mapping?
A. $f(x) = 34 - x^4$
B. $f(x) = 4x^2 + 2$
C. $f(x) = x^4 + 2$
D. $f(x) = x^2 + 14$

RELATIONS, FUNCTIONS & ARITHMATIC SEQUENCE

33. $f(x) = \frac{x-5}{2}$

    Which mapping best represents the above function?

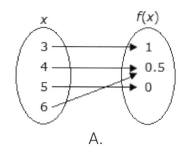
A.

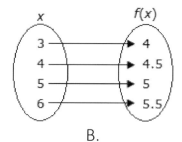
B.

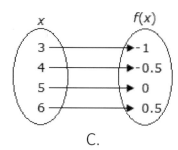
C.

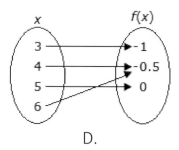
D.

34. $f(x) = -x^2 + 4$

    Which mapping does NOT represent the above function? Select all that apply.

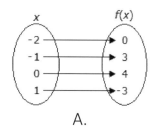
A.

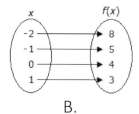
B.

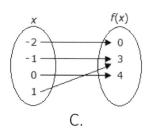
C.

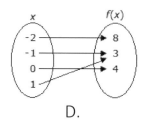
D.

RELATIONS, FUNCTIONS & ARITHMATIC SEQUENCE

35. Given this graph of the function f(x):

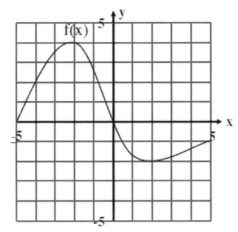

Find x when f(x) = 0

A. 0
B. -5
C. Both A and B
D. None

36. Jessica works at restaurant where she gets paid $7.00 an hour. She works between 15 and 35 hours every week. Her weekly salary can be modeled by the equation, S = 7h, where S is her weekly salary and h is the number of hours she worked in a week.

    What is the minimum value of range in this scenario?

37. Complete the following statement by selecting ONE answer from each box for the sequence : −8, −16, −32, −64, …

    To find the next number
    A. Add
    B. Subtract
    C. Multiply
    D. Divide

    the previous term by
    A. 2
    B. -2
    C. -8
    D. 5

    And next two numbers obtained are
    A. -128, -256
    B. -72, -80
    C. -56, -48
    D. 128, 256

RELATIONS, FUNCTIONS & ARITHMATIC SEQUENCE

38. A formula in which the *n*th term of a sequence is expressed in terms of the previous term, as in is called what?

    A. exponential
    B. geometric
    C. recursive
    D. explicit

39. Which sequence uses the algebraic expression $6n + 7$ to describe the relationship between a term in the sequence and its position, n, in the sequence?

    A. 7, 9, 14, 19, 24 ...
    B. 4, 8, 12, 16, 20 ...
    C. 13, 19, 25, 31 ...
    D. 9, 10, 11, 12, 13 ...

40. A sequence can be generated by using $a_n = 3a_{(n-1)}$, where $a_1 = 7$ and *n* is a whole number greater than 1. What are the first four terms in the sequence?

    A. 7, 24, 96, 384
    B. 7, 10, 14, 18
    C. 7, 21, 63, 189
    D. 7, 20, 76, 300

RELATIONS, FUNCTIONS & ARITHMATIC SEQUENCE

41. The graph of which of following scenarios would be discrete?
    A. The height h, in inches, of a student depends on the student's age, a, in years.
    B. The time t, in seconds, it takes a runner to finish a race depends on the distance in miles m of the race.
    C. The number of students taking a test n depends on the number of students in the class c.
    D. The length l, in feet, of a walkway depends on the number of bricks b used.

42. Write a function to represent the sequence listed below.
    2, 7, 12, 17, 22, 27
    A. f(x) = 3x + 1
    B. f(x) = 5x - 3
    C. f(x) = x + 5
    D. f(x) = 7x − 2

43. A sequence is created from the function k(n) = 2n + 3, where n represents the position of the term of the sequence. The sequence does not begin at 0. Which list represents the first five terms of the sequence?
    A. 3, 5, 7, 9, 11
    B. 5, 7, 9, 11, 13
    C. 5, 9, 13, 17, 21
    D. 2, 3, 4, 5, 6

RELATIONS, FUNCTIONS & ARITHMATIC SEQUENCE

44. The table shows the cost of shipping t-shirts, c(t), based on the number of t-shirts ordered, t.

Number of shirts ordered t	Total cost of shipping t-shirts, c(t)
1	$2.50
2	$2.80
3	$3.10
4	$3.40
5	$3.70
6	$4.00
7	$4.30
8	$4.60

    The pattern in the table continues. Which value represents the cost of shipping 12 t-shirts?
    A. $4.90
    B. $5.20
    C. $5.50
    D. $5.80

45. The sum of the interior angles of a triangle is 180º, of a quadrilateral is 360° and of a pentagon is 540º. Assuming this pattern continues, find the sum of the interior angles of a decagon (10 sides).
    A. 1000°
    B. 1440°
    C. 1800°
    D. 2160°

RELATIONS, FUNCTIONS & ARITHMATIC SEQUENCE

46. Which term of the arithmetic sequence -3, 2, 7, ... would give you 117?
    A. 25
    B. 17
    C. 10
    D. 28

47. Use the recursive formula to find the fourth term of the sequence.
    $$f(n) = 3f(n - 1) - 4$$
    $$f(1) = 5$$
    A. 29
    B. 1
    C. 11
    D. 83

48. Which term of the arithmetic sequence -9, -6, -3 ... would give you 87?
    A. 30
    B. 33
    C. 249
    D. 230

49. Which term of the arithmetic sequence 31, 27, 23... would give you -17? Record your answer in the space provided below.

RELATIONS, FUNCTIONS & ARITHMATIC SEQUENCE

50. If $a_{12} = 28.6$, d = 1.8 in arithmetic sequence, what will be its 4th term?
    A. 13.8
    B. 14.2
    C. 15.6
    D. 16.9

51. If $a_{18} = 27.4$, d = 1.1 in arithmetic sequence, what will be its first term?
    A. 2.4
    B. 8.3
    C. 7.6
    D. 8.7

52. Given the nth term and common difference of an arithmetic sequence, it is possible to find the (n+1)th term. Circle one answer.
                   TRUE   FALSE

53. An employee is offered a $40,000 starting salary with an annual raise of $600. What will be his salary in 12th year?
    A. 46,000
    B. 46,600
    C. 47,200
    D. None of above

RELATIONS, FUNCTIONS & ARITHMATIC SEQUENCE

54. Which of the situation shows an example of discrete graph?
    A. Dog's weight
    B. Number of students in class
    C. A person height
    D. All of the above

55. The surface area of a cube can be found using the following formula: $A = 6s^2$, where A represents the surface area of the cube and s represents the length of one edge. Your geometry teacher wants you to draw a cube that has a length of at least 3 inches.
    What is the domain for this problem?
    A. {3}
    B. $x \leq 3$
    C. $x \geq 3$
    D. can't determine

56. Which of the following tables does not represent a fun?

    A.
x	1	4	-1	-4
y	2	1	2	1

    B.
x	1	-2	3	1
y	1	4	9	16

    C.
x	-1	3	2	5
y	-1	3	2	5

    D.
x	2	1	3	4
y	0	1	5	0

RELATIONS, FUNCTIONS & ARITHMATIC SEQUENCE

57. If $f(x) = \frac{x}{2x+1}$, $x \in R$, find $f\left(\frac{1}{5}\right)$

    A. $\frac{1}{5}$

    B. $\frac{2}{5}$

    C. $\frac{1}{7}$

    D. 7

58. If $g(x) = x - 2x^2$, find $g(-8)$.

    A. -136

    B. 120

    C. -40

    D. 24

59. Solve $y = mx + b$ for m.

    A. $m = \frac{y-b}{x}$

    B. $m = \frac{x}{y-b}$

    C. $m = y + bx$

    D. $m = \frac{y+b}{x}$

RELATIONS, FUNCTIONS & ARITHMATIC SEQUENCE

60. Mary collected data on the ages and heights of a random sample of third, fifth, and eighth grade students at her school. If she plots the data on a scatter plot, what relationship will she most likely see between age and height?

    A. A negative correlation
    B. A constant correlation
    C. A positive correlation
    D. no correlation

RELATIONS, FUNCTIONS & ARITHMATIC SEQUENCE

Answer Key – Relations, Functions & Arithmetic Sequence

		Marks (C/W)			Marks (C/W)
1	D		31	-10	
2	B		32	C	
3	B		33	C	
4	-193		34	A, B, D	
5	C		35	C	
6	A		36	105	
7	C		37	C, A, A	
8	C		38	C	
9	D		39	C	
10	A, A, B, B, A, A		40	C	
11	A		41	C	
12	A		42	B	
13	C		43	B	
14	C		44	D	
15	B, E		45	B	
16	B, D, F		46	A	
17	B		47	D	
18	B		48	B	
19	C		49	13	
20	B		50	B	
21	B		51	D	
22	A, D		52	TRUE	
23	B		53	B	
24	A		54	B	
25	B		55	C	
26	A, E		56	B	
27	C		57	C	
28	A		58	A	
29	C		59	A	
30	B		60	C	
	Total			Total	

SECTION 3

DIFFERENT FORMS OF LINEAR EQUATIONS

DIFFERENT FORMS OF LINEAR EQUATIONS

1. Find the x- and y-intercepts.

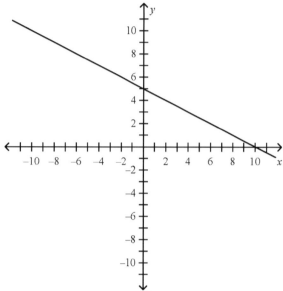

A. x-intercept: −10, y-intercept: 5
B. x-intercept: 5, y-intercept: 10
C. x-intercept: 10, y-intercept: −5
D. x-intercept: 10, y-intercept: 5

2. Determine the value of r so that the line through (5, 2) and (7, r) has a slope of 3. Record your answer in the space provided below.

DIFFERENT FORMS OF LINEAR EQUATIONS

3. Which graph is the graph of 3(y - 3) = -2x?

A.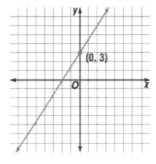

B.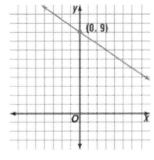

C.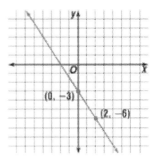

D.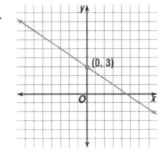

4. Find the slope of the line that passes through (-2, 9.5) and (4, 5).

    A. $\frac{3}{4}$

    B. $-\frac{3}{4}$

    C. 0

    D. undefined

DIFFERENT FORMS OF LINEAR EQUATIONS

5. What is the equation of the line shown in the graph?

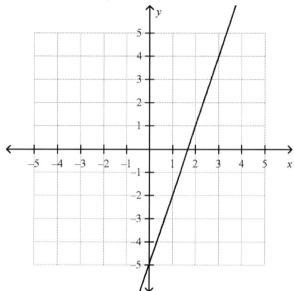

A. $y = 3x + \frac{3}{2}$
B. $y = -3x - 5$
C. $y = 3x - 5$
D. $y = 2x - 5$

DIFFERENT FORMS OF LINEAR EQUATIONS

6. What is the slope of $\overline{AB}$ in parallelogram *ABCD*?

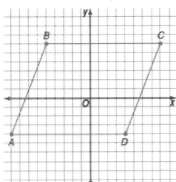

A. $-\dfrac{5}{2}$

B. $\dfrac{5}{2}$

C. $\dfrac{2}{5}$

D. $-\dfrac{2}{5}$

7. Which of the following graph has equation $2y + 3x + 6 = 0$?

A.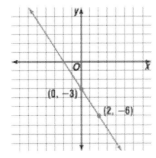

B.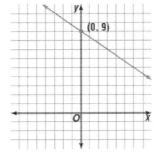

C.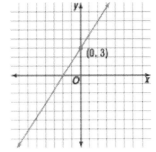

D.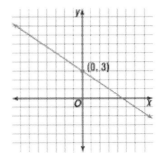

DIFFERENT FORMS OF LINEAR EQUATIONS

8. Which of the following pairs of coordinates are on a line with an undefined slope?
   A. (-4, -3), (3, -3)
   B. (2, 1), (5, -2)
   C. (3, -2), (3, 5)
   D. (-2, -2), (4, 4)

9. Which of the following pairs of coordinates are on a line with zero slope?
   A. (-1, -8), (3, -8)
   B. (4, 1), (5, -2)
   C. (3, -9), (3, 5)
   D. (-2, 0), (4, 1)

10. Find x-intercept of the line which has slope $\frac{1}{2}$ and y-intercept 3. Record your answer in the space provided below.

DIFFERENT FORMS OF LINEAR EQUATIONS

11. Select one correct answer from each of the box below.

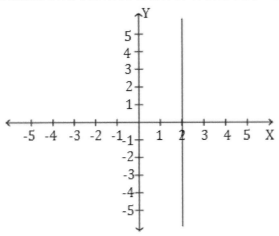

Above graph has
- ○ Zero
- ○ Undefined
- ○ 1
- ○ 2

slope and equation is given by,

- A. Y = 2x
- B. Y = 2
- C. X = 2

12. Which of the following is the equation of the line that has x-intercept = −2 and y-intercept = −4?

A. $y = -2x - 4$
B. $y = 2x - 4$
C. $y = -2x + 4$
D. $y = -\frac{1}{2}x - 4$

DIFFERENT FORMS OF LINEAR EQUATIONS

13. Find value of 'm' for the line that contains the points (m, m−1) and (m−2, 8) and slope is $-\frac{7}{3}$

   A. −5
   B. 3
   C. $-\frac{7}{5}$
   D. $\frac{13}{3}$

14. Reserved tickets for the football game cost $20 each and general admission tickets cost $12 each. The total ticket sales brought in $900. The equation below can be used to find out how many of each type of ticket were sold, where x is the number of reserved tickets and y is the number of general admission tickets.

$$20x + 12y = 900$$

Which of the following graphs shows the graph of this equation?

A.

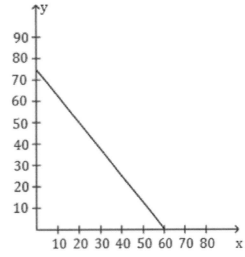

B.

C.

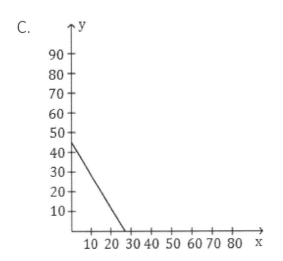

D.

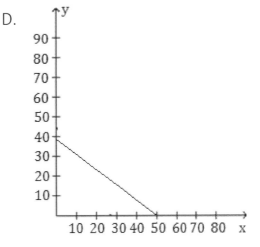

DIFFERENT FORMS OF LINEAR EQUATIONS

15. Which of the following graphs shows the graph of this equation?

$$y + 1 = 2(x - 1)$$

A.
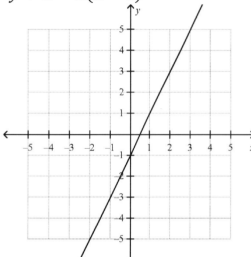

C.
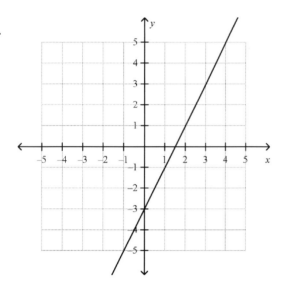

B.
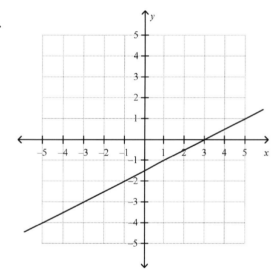

D.
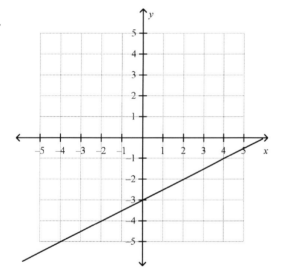

16. The scatter plot shows the relationship between the weekly total sales ($) and the number of different rugs designs a rug store has. Based on this relationship, use the line of best fit to predict. What the total sales will be when the store has 110 different rug designs.

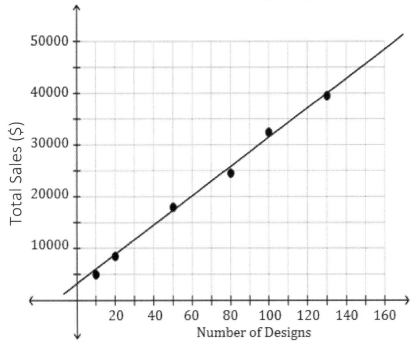

A. $31,000
B. $0
C. $38,000
D. $35,000

DIFFERENT FORMS OF LINEAR EQUATIONS

17. The values in the table show a linear relationship. Find the slope.

x	-4	2	8	14
y	10	7	4	1

    A. 2
    B. −2
    C. $\frac{1}{2}$
    D. $-\frac{1}{2}$

18. Find the equation of line where it crosses x-axis at -3 and y-axis at 4.
    A. Y = -3x + 4
    B. 4x − 3y + 12 = 0
    C. -3x + 4y = 0
    D. -3x + 4y = 12

19. What is the slope and y-intercept of a line which represent the data in the table?

x	1	2	3	4	5
y	-3	-2	-1	0	1

    Slope   A. 0.25   B. 1   C. 4   D. 0

    Y intercept   E. -3   F. -4   G. 4   H. None

    Select one answers from each box. Select all applicable answers:

DIFFERENT FORMS OF LINEAR EQUATIONS

20. Ben is training for a marathon. Part of his training is a "walk/run" session where he walks for *x* minutes and runs for *y* minutes for a total distance of 3000 meters. His walking speed is 110 meters per minute. His running speed is 220 meters per minute. This situation can be represented by the following equation:

    $110x + 220y = 3000$

    Above equation is in [○ Slope intercept / ○ Point slope / ○ Standard] form and has a slope of

    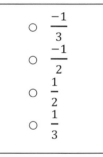

    - ○ $\frac{-1}{3}$
    - ○ $\frac{-1}{2}$
    - ○ $\frac{1}{2}$
    - ○ $\frac{1}{3}$

21. Write an equation for the line that has a *y*-intercept of 2 and is perpendicular to the line $3x + y = 6$.
    A. $y = -3x + 2$
    B. $y = -3x - 2$
    C. $y = \frac{1}{3}x + 2$
    D. $y = -\frac{1}{3}x + 2$

DIFFERENT FORMS OF LINEAR EQUATIONS

22. The temperature of air in a room that began at 55°F is increasing by 8°F per hour. The following equation represents this situation:

$y = 55 + 8x$

Where x represents the number of hours and y represents the temperature.

Which of the following is a graph of this equation?

A.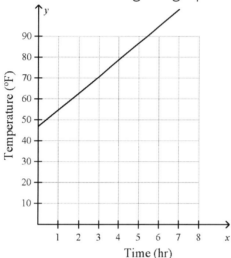

C.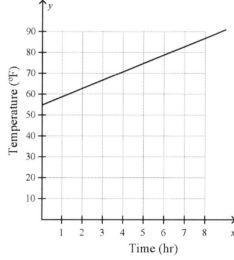

B.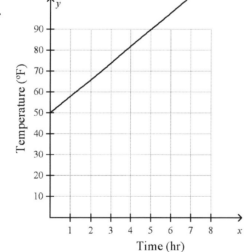

D.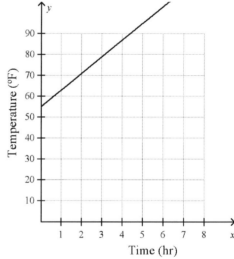

DIFFERENT FORMS OF LINEAR EQUATIONS

23. Write an equation in slope-intercept form for the line that passes through (3, 7) and (7, 4).

A. $y = -\frac{3}{4}x + \frac{37}{4}$

B. $y = \frac{3}{4}x + \frac{37}{4}$

C. $y = -\frac{4}{3}x + \frac{37}{4}$

D. $y = -\frac{3}{4}x + \frac{4}{37}$

DIFFERENT FORMS OF LINEAR EQUATIONS

24. Graph the line described by the equation $-2x - 4y = 16$.

A.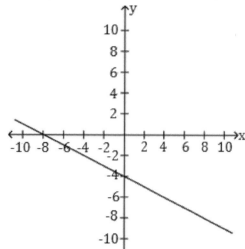

C.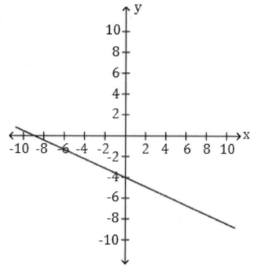

B.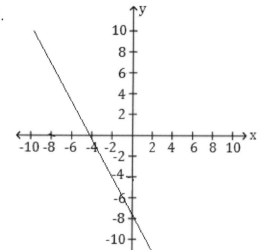

D.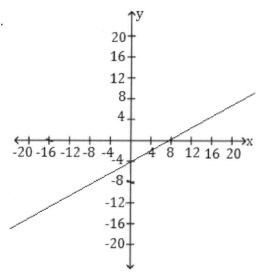

25. Find the value of k so that line has a slope of 5 and passes through the point (k, 2k+1) and (-1, -k).

DIFFERENT FORMS OF LINEAR EQUATIONS

26. Simon is building new apartments. The graph below shows the relation in price of apartment and its height.

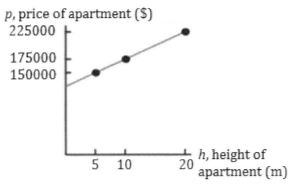

What is the equation of this linear function? What is the slope and what does it represent?

A. $y = -500x + 125,000$; slope = -500; this means that for every meter rise of apartment, $500 is the amount to be given apart from 125,000 as initial amount

B. $y = 5000x + 125,000$; slope = 5000; this means that for every meter rise of apartment, $5000 is the amount to be given apart from 125,000 as initial amount

C. $y = 2500x + 125,000$; slope = 2,500; this means that for every meter rise of apartment, $5000 is the amount to be given apart from 125,000 as initial amount

D. $y = 25x + 125,000$; slope = 25; this means that for every meter rise of apartment, $5,000 is the amount to be given apart from 125,000 as initial amount

27. Find the x-intercept of line which has slope 2 and passes through the point A (3,1).

DIFFERENT FORMS OF LINEAR EQUATIONS

28. Alyssa is enrolled in a public-speaking class. Each week she is required to give a speech of greater length than the speech she gave the week before. The table below shows the lengths of several of her speeches.

    Alyssa's Speeches

Week Number	3	4	5	6
Length of Speech (seconds)	150	180	210	240

    If this trend continues, in which week will she give a 12-minute speech?
    A. 22
    B. 12
    C. 15
    D. 24

29. What is the slope of the line which is parallel and perpendicular to line $2x - 5y = 10$?
    Select one answer for each box.

A $\frac{2}{5}$	B 5	C $\frac{-1}{5}$	D $\frac{-5}{2}$

    Parallel Line Slope   A   B   C   D

    Perpendicular Line Slope   A   B   C   D

DIFFERENT FORMS OF LINEAR EQUATIONS

30. Jorge graphed the line shown below. What is the slope of line which is perpendicular to line below?

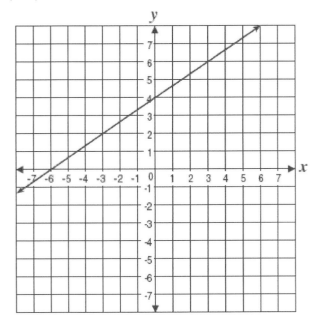

A. $\dfrac{2}{3}$

B. $-\dfrac{2}{3}$

C. $-\dfrac{3}{2}$

D. $\dfrac{3}{2}$

31. Given the equation:

$y = -3$

What is the slope? What is the y-intercept?

A. Slope = -3; y-intercept = -3

B. Slope is undefined; y-intercept = -3

C. Slope = 0; y-intercept = 0

D. Slope = 0; y-intercept = -3

DIFFERENT FORMS OF LINEAR EQUATIONS

32. Abbey goes bike riding. The graph represents the distance she rides over time. Which of the following is the best interpretation of the slope of the line segment? Select ONE answer in each row.

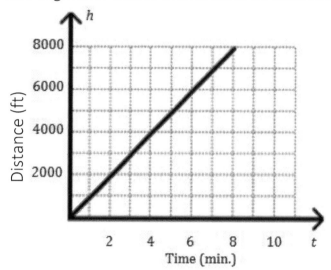

Statement	True	False
She rides bike 1,000 feet per minute.	A	B
It takes her 1 minute to ride 2,000 feet.	A	B
She will ride 10,000 ft in 10 min.	A	B
It takes her 2 minute to ride 2,000 feet.	A	B
Slope can't be determined.	A	B

DIFFERENT FORMS OF LINEAR EQUATIONS

33. Charlie has $75 saved and wants to buy DVDs, which cost $9.00 per DVD. The linear equation $y = -9x + 75$ represents this situation where y is the number of dollars remaining from his savings and x is the number of DVDs that have been purchased.

    What is the x-intercept? What does the x-intercept represent?

    A. x-intercept = 75; The x-intercept represents the amount of money Charlie has saved.

    B. x-intercept = 8; The x-intercept represents the number of DVDs that Charlie can buy. In this case this means he can buy 8 DVDs.

    C. x-intercept = $\frac{25}{3}$; The x-intercept represents the number of DVDs that Charlie can buy. In this case this means he can buy 8 DVDs.

    D. x-intercept = 3; The x-intercept represents the amount of money Charlie has left after he has purchased 8 DVDs.

DIFFERENT FORMS OF LINEAR EQUATIONS

34. Miguel has $85 saved and wants to buy DVDs, which cost $8.50 per DVD. The linear equation $y = -8.50x + 85$ represents the number of dollars y remaining from his savings after x DVDs have been purchased. Explain the meaning of the slope as a rate of change.

    A. The slope means that Miguel spends $8.50 from his savings for every DVD he buys. The slope is negative, because the amount in his savings is decreasing.
    B. The slope means that Miguel spends $8.50 from his savings for every DVD he buys. The slope is positive, because the amount Miguel is spending is increasing.
    C. The slope means that Miguel spends $8.50 from his savings for every DVD he buys. The slope is positive, because the amount Miguel is spending is increasing.
    D. The slope means that Miguel spends $7.50 from his savings for every DVD he buys. The slope is negative, because the amount Miguel is spending is increasing.

DIFFERENT FORMS OF LINEAR EQUATIONS

35. Find the slope of the line that contains (1, 6) and (1, -9).
    A. Slope = 0
    B. Slope = 1
    C. Slope is undefined
    D. Not enough information

36. Jane is in debt. She owes her brother money and has nothing in her piggy bank. She decides to work odd jobs for her family and neighbors to build her savings back up. The graph below represents Jane's situation.

    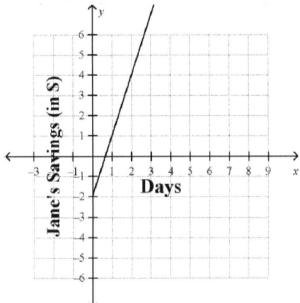

    What is the equation of this linear function? What does the slope represent?
    A. $y = 3x - 2$; The slope of 3 means Jane will be saving $3 every day.
    B. $y = 3x + 2$; The slope of mean it will take Jane 3 days to save a dollar.
    C. $y = -3x - 2$; The slope of -2 means Jane was $2 in debt to her brother.
    D. $y = x - 2$; The slope of 1 means Jane will be saving $1 every day.

DIFFERENT FORMS OF LINEAR EQUATIONS

37. Which of the following is the equation of the line that has x-intercept = 7 and y-intercept = −2?

    A. $y - 2 = \frac{2}{7}(x - 0)$
    B. $y + 2 = \frac{2}{7}(x - 0)$
    C. $y + 2 = -\frac{2}{7}(x - 0)$
    D. $y - 2 = -\frac{2}{7}(x - 0)$

38. Find the equation of the line that passes through the points (a, 2a) and (2a, a).

    A. $y = -x + 3a$
    B. $y = -x - 3a$
    C. $y = x + 3a$
    D. $y = x - 3a$

DIFFERENT FORMS OF LINEAR EQUATIONS

39. Graph the line with the slope $\frac{3}{2}$ and y-intercept 1.

A.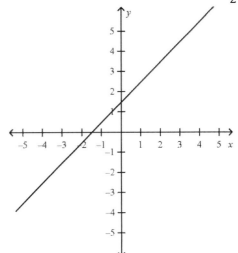

C.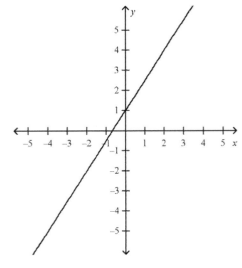

B.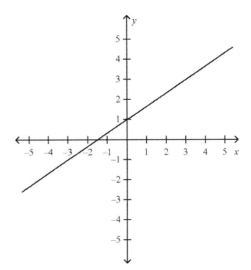

D.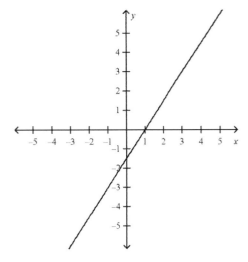

40. Write an equation in standard form for the line that passes through (4, 4) and has a x-intercept of 3.

    A. $4x - y - 12 = 0$
    B. $y - \frac{1}{4}x - 12 = 0$
    C. $y - 4x - 12 = 0$
    D. $y + 4x + 12 = 0$

41. Refer the graph below and select ONE answer in each row.

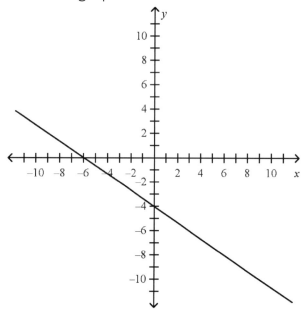

Statement	True	False
Slope of given line is $\frac{2}{3}$.	A	B
Range of given line is all real numbers.	A	B
Standard form of equation is 2x + 3y = -12.	A	B
Line is passing through (9,-11).	A	B
It is an increasing function.	A	B

DIFFERENT FORMS OF LINEAR EQUATIONS

42. The ordered pairs (20, -29.5), (21, -31), and (22, -32.5) are points on the graph of a linear equation.

    Which of the following graphs show all the ordered pairs in the solution set of this linear equation?

    A.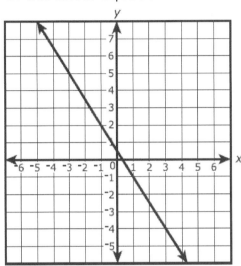

    B.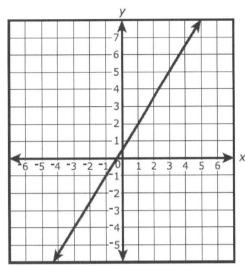

    C.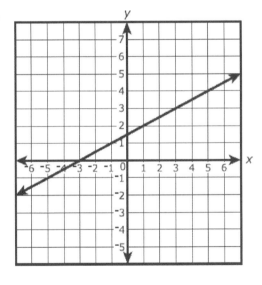

    D.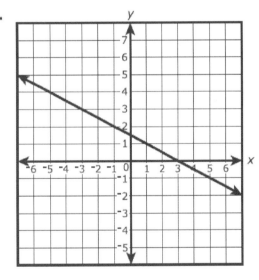

43.

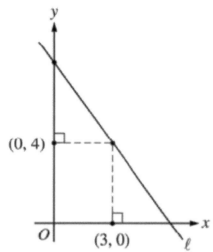

Note: Figure not drawn to scale.

In the figure above, if line *l* has a slope of –2, what is the y-intercept of *l*?
A. 4
B. 8
C. 9
D. 10

44.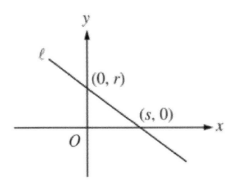

In the figure above, what is the slope of line *l*?

A. $-\dfrac{r}{s}$

B. $\dfrac{r}{s}$

C. $-\dfrac{s}{r}$

D. $\dfrac{s}{r}$

45. What is the slope of the line which is perpendicular to line $5x - 12y = 24$?

A. -2

B. $\dfrac{-12}{5}$

C. -12

D. $\dfrac{5}{12}$

DIFFERENT FORMS OF LINEAR EQUATIONS

46. What is the equation in slope-intercept form of the line that passes through the points (-4, 47) and (2, -16)?

A. $y = -\frac{21}{2}x + \frac{979}{21}$

B. $y = -\frac{2}{21}x + \frac{979}{21}$

C. $y = -\frac{21}{2}x + 5$

D. $y = -\frac{2}{21}x + 5$

47. The graph models the linear relationship between the temperature of Earth's atmosphere and the altitude above sea level.

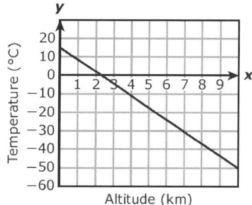

Earth's Atmosphere

Which of these bests represents the rate of change of the temperature with respect to altitude?

A. $-6.6°C/km$

B. $-3.5°C/km$

C. $-0.29°C/km$

D. $-0.15°C/km$

DIFFERENT FORMS OF LINEAR EQUATIONS

48. Find y intercept of following equation.
$$\frac{-5}{6}x + \frac{11}{3}y = -11$$

Write your answer in the space below.

49. Select the statements which are true for the line that passes through the point (2, 7) and has a slope of zero.
    A. Line is parallel to x-axis.
    B. Line is parallel to y-axis.
    C. Y-intercept can't be identified from the given information.
    D. There is no x-intercept.
    E. Line is passing through (0,7) also.

50. The table represents some points on the graph of a linear function.

x	y
-20	-268
-14	-196
-8	-124
-1	-40

    Which equation represents the same relationship?
    A. $y + 268 = \frac{1}{12}(x + 20)$
    B. $y + 20 = \frac{1}{12}(x + 268)$
    C. $y + 268 = 12(x + 20)$
    D. $y + 20 = 12(x + 268)$

DIFFERENT FORMS OF LINEAR EQUATIONS

51. The function $y = 3.75 + 1.5(x - 1)$ can be used to determine the cost in dollars for a taxi ride of x miles. What is the rate of change of the cost in dollars with respect to the number of miles?

    A. $1.50 per mile
    B. $3.75 per mile
    C. $4.25 per mile
    D. $5.25 per mile

52. A student graphed $f(x) = x$ and $g(x) = f(x) + 3$ on the same coordinate grid. Which statements describe how the graphs of f and g are related? Select all the applicable answers.

    A. The graph of f is shifted 3 units up to create the graph of g.
    B. The graph of f is steeper than the graph of g.
    C. The graph of f is shifted 3 units down to create the graph of g.
    D. The slope of the graph f and g is same.
    E. F and g intersect exactly at one point.
    F. Range for both the functions are same.

DIFFERENT FORMS OF LINEAR EQUATIONS

53. The graph of linear function g is shown on the grid.

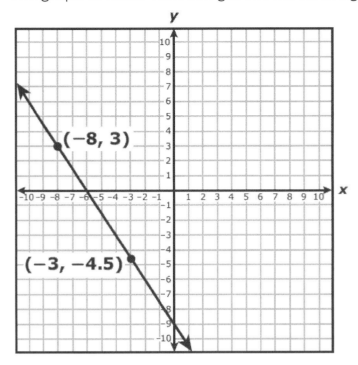

Determine the equation in point slope form.

A. $y - 3 = \frac{3}{2}(x - 8)$

B. $y - 3 = \frac{-3}{2}(x - 8)$

C. $y + 3 = \frac{3}{2}(x - 8)$

D. $y - 3 = -\frac{3}{2}(x + 8)$

54. Which value of x makes the equation $0.75(x + 20) = 2 + 0.5(x - 2)$ true? Record the answer in the space provided below.

55. A lifeguard earns $320 per week for working 40 hours plus $12 per hour worked over 40 hours. A lifeguard can work a maximum of 60 hours per week.

Which graph best represents the lifeguard's weekly earnings in dollars for working h hours over 40?

A.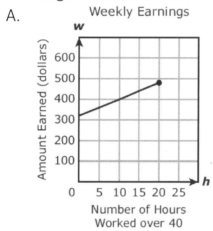

C.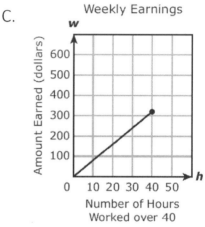

B.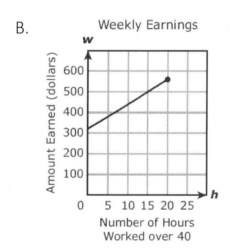

D.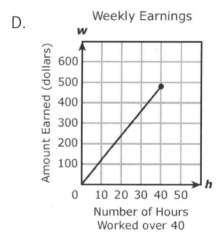

DIFFERENT FORMS OF LINEAR EQUATIONS

56. What is the equation of the line shown in the graph?

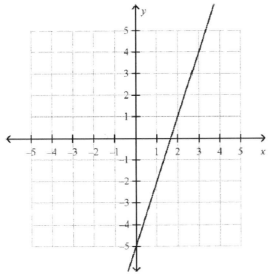

A. $y = 3x + \frac{3}{2}$
B. $y = -3x - 5$
C. $y = 3x - 5$
D. $y = 2x - 5$

57. When independent variable increases dependent variable remains same then the slope is _____.

A. Positive
B. Negative
C. Zero
D. undefined

58. Which of the following graphs shows the graph of this equation
$$y + 1 = -2(1 - x)$$

A.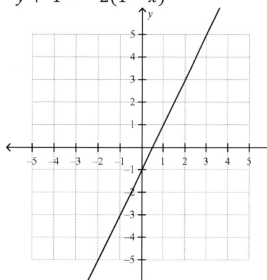

C.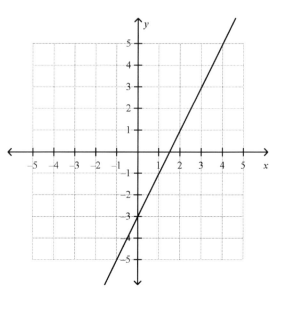

B.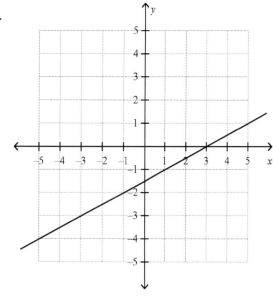

D.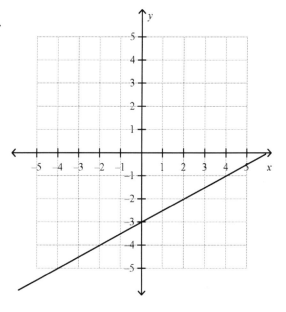

DIFFERENT FORMS OF LINEAR EQUATIONS

59. Graph the line described by the equation $x + 2y + 16 = 0$.

A.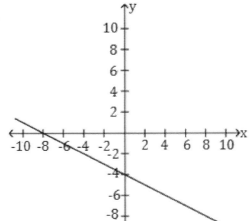

C.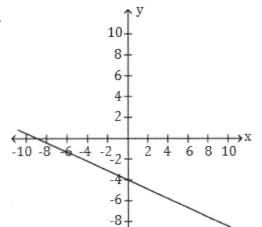

B.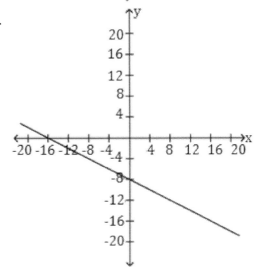

D.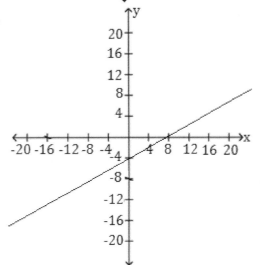

DIFFERENT FORMS OF LINEAR EQUATIONS

60. Sarah is going shopping for shirts and sweaters. Shirt cost $6 and sweater cost $9. Sarah will spend $54. The equation below can be used to find out how many shirts and sweaters she can buy, where x is the number of shirts and y is the number of sweaters.

$6x + 9y = 54$

Which of the following graphs shows the graph of this equation?

A.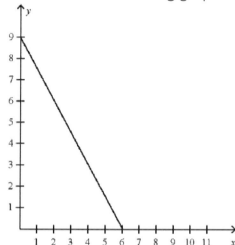

C.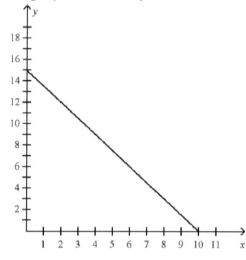

B.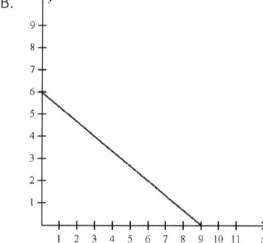

D.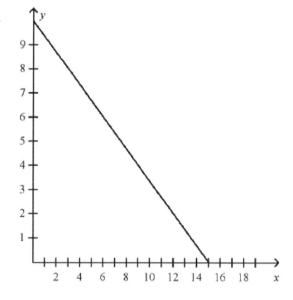

DIFFERENT FORMS OF LINEAR EQUATIONS

61. When the dependent variable decreases as the independent variable increase, the rate of change is
    A. Positive
    B. Negative
    C. Zero
    D. Undefined

62. Write standard form of the equation of the line which passes through (-4, -5) and perpendicular to y = x - 4.
    A. $-x - y - 9 = 0$
    B. $x + y - 9 = 0$
    C. $-x - y + 9 = 0$
    D. $x - y - 9 = 0$

63. What is the slope and equation of a line passes through (-3, 3) and parallel to $y = 0$. Select one correct answer from each box below.

    A. -1
    B. Undefined
    C. 0

    D. X = -3
    E. Y = 3
    F. None

    Slope   Equation of line

64. Write the equation of line passes through (-7, -8) and parallel to $y = 0$.
    A. x = 8
    B. y = -8
    C. x = -8
    D. y = 8

DIFFERENT FORMS OF LINEAR EQUATIONS

65. Write the equation of line passes through (2,3) and perpendicular to $y = 0$.
    A. y = 2
    B. x = -2
    C. y = -2
    D. x = 2

66. Find the slope of line which is perpendicular to x = -2.
    A. 1
    B. 0
    C. -1
    D. 2

67. Write the standard form of the equation of the line which passes through (1, -1) and perpendicular to $y = -6x + 9$.
    A. $6x + y - 7 = 0$
    B. $x + 6y - 7 = 0$
    C. $x - 6y - 7 = 0$
    D. $6y + x + 7 = 0$

DIFFERENT FORMS OF LINEAR EQUATIONS

68. Write slope intercept form of the equation of the line which passes through (4, -5) and parallel to y = $-\frac{5}{2}$x -7.

    A. $y = -\frac{5}{2}x + 5$
    B. $y = \frac{5}{2}x - 5$
    C. $y = -\frac{5}{2}x - 5$
    D. $y = \frac{5}{2}x + 5$

69. Which of the following lines is perpendicular to the line y = −7?

    A. $y = \frac{1}{5}x + 3$
    B. y + 3 = −5(x + 2)
    C. y = 7
    D. x = −3

70. Write an equation for the line that has a y-intercept of 7 and is perpendicular to the line 4x + 3y = 8.

    A. y = −3x + 7
    B. y = −4x − 2
    C. $y = \frac{3}{4}x + 7$
    D. $y = -\frac{4}{3}x + 7$

DIFFERENT FORMS OF LINEAR EQUATIONS

71. Find the equation of line which is passing through (-3, 5) and parallel to y = -x+ 6
    A. y = -x + 4
    B. y= -2x + 5
    C. 2y = -x + 6
    D. Y = -x + 2

72. Find the equation of line which is perpendicular to $\frac{5}{4}(x-1) = \frac{1}{3}y$ and has y intercept 5.
    A. y = $\frac{-2x}{15}$ + 10
    B. y = $\frac{-4x}{20}$ + 5
    C. y = $\frac{-4x}{15}$ + 5
    D. y = $\frac{2x}{15}$ + 10

73. Write the equation of line passes through (-7, 3) and parallel to y =0.
    Record your answer in the space provided below.

DIFFERENT FORMS OF LINEAR EQUATIONS

74. Write the equation of line passes through (-3, -5) and perpendicular to y =0.

    A. y = 3
    B. x = -3
    C. y = -5
    D. x = 5

75. Find the equation of line which is passing through (-2, -8) and parallel to 2y = x − 4.

    A. $y = \frac{x}{2} - 7$
    B. $y = \frac{3x}{2} - 4$
    C. $2y = \frac{x}{2} - 8$
    D. $y = \frac{x}{8} - 7$

76. Find the statements which are not TRUE for a line which is perpendicular to 3y + 4x − 2 = 0 and has x-intercept -3. Select all applicable answers.

    A. Given equation is in standard form.
    B. Slope of a line perpendicular to the line is $\frac{-4}{3}$
    C. Y intercept of a line perpendicular to the line is $\frac{9}{4}$
    D. Y intercept of given line is $\frac{-2}{3}$
    E. Given line is steeper than the perpendicular line.

DIFFERENT FORMS OF LINEAR EQUATIONS

77. Write the equation of line which passes through (-5, 5) and parallel to y =0.
    A. y=-5
    B. x=5
    C. y =5
    D. x =-5

78. Which of the following lines is perpendicular to the line $x = -5$?
    A. $y = \frac{1}{5}x + 3$
    B. $y + 3 = -5(x + 2)$
    C. $y = 5$
    D. $x = -5$

79. Write the equation of line passes through (-7 -4) and perpendicular to y =0.
    A. x =-7
    B. y=7
    C. x =7
    D. y = -7

80. The equation of line 'j' is $6x + 5y = 3$, and the equation of line 'q' is $5x - 6y = 0$. Which statement about the two lines is true?
    A. Lines j and q have the same y-intercept.
    B. Lines j and q are parallel.
    C. Lines j and q have the same x-intercept.
    D. Lines j and q are perpendicular.

81. Which is the line parallel to the line y = 8x-2?
    A. $y = 2x - 8$
    B. $y = -\frac{1}{8x} + 3$
    C. $y = 4 + 8x$
    D. $2y = 8x + 3$

82. Find an equation for the line with y-intercept 3 that is perpendicular to the line 3y = 2x − 4.
    A. $2y = 6 - 3x$
    B. $2y = 3x + 6$
    C. $3y = 9 - 2x$
    D. $3y = 2x + 9$

83. Which equations of a line can be parallel to line $\overleftrightarrow{MN}$? Select more than one applicable answers.

    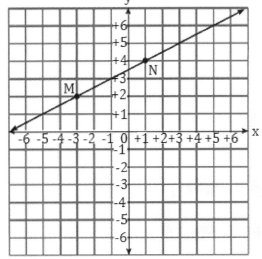

    A. $2x - y = 3$
    B. $x - 2y = 3$
    C. $8x + 4y = 4$
    D. $9x + 18y = -9$
    E. $x = 2y$
    F. $6x - 3y = 0$

DIFFERENT FORMS OF LINEAR EQUATIONS

84. What is the equation of the line that is perpendicular to $\overline{PQ}$ and passes through the origin?

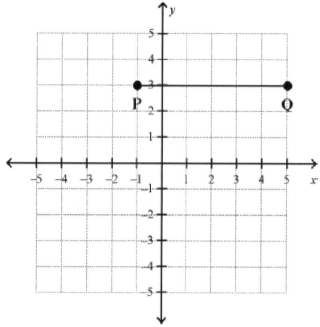

A. $y = -1$
B. $x = 0$
C. $y = 0$
D. $y = x$

85. Write an equation for the line that contains the point (-1, 3) and is perpendicular to the line y = 5.

A. $x + y = -1$
B. $x + y = 1$
C. $y = 2$
D. $x = -1$

DIFFERENT FORMS OF LINEAR EQUATIONS

86. Write an equation for the line that contains the point (-1, 2) and is perpendicular to the line given below.

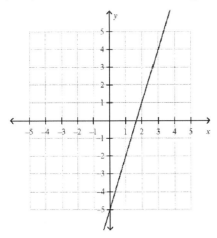

A. $x + 3y = 5$
B. $x + 3y = 1$
C. $y = 3x + 5$
D. $y = 3x - 5$

87. What is the equation of line which is parallel to given line below?

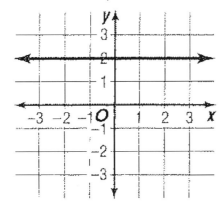

A. y = x + 2

B. y = -7

C. x = -5

D. x = 2

DIFFERENT FORMS OF LINEAR EQUATIONS

88. What is the equation of line shown in the graph?

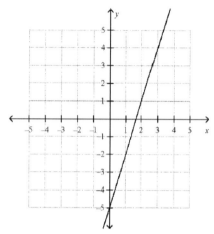

A. $y = 3x + \frac{3}{2}$

B. $y = -3x - 5$

C. $y = 3x - 5$

D. $y = 2x - 5$

89. Solve $7(x - 2) = 7x + 14$.

A. no solution

B. 0

C. 2

D. All real numbers

DIFFERENT FORMS OF LINEAR EQUATIONS

90. A clothing manufacturer needs 2.4 yards of fabric to make a jacket and 1.6 yards of fabric to make a matching skirt. The number of jackets, x, and skirts, y, that can be made from a 48-yard bolt of fabric can be represented by the equation $2.4x + 1.6y = 48$. Graph the function and find its intercepts. What does each intercept represent?

A.
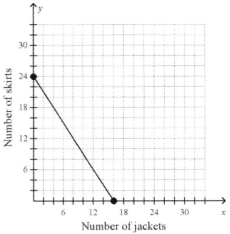

B.
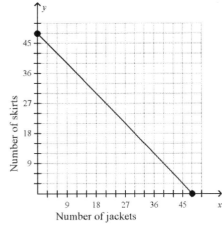

The x-intercept is (16, 0). The x-intercept gives the total number of skirts that can be made from one bolt of fabric when only skirts are made.

The y-intercept is (0, 24). The y-intercept gives the total number of jackets that can be made from one bolt of fabric when only jackets are made.

The x-intercept is (48, 0). The x-intercept gives the total number of jackets that can be made from one bolt of fabric when only jackets are made.

The y-intercept is (0, 48). The y-intercept gives the total number of skirts that can be made from one bolt of fabric when only skirts are made.

C.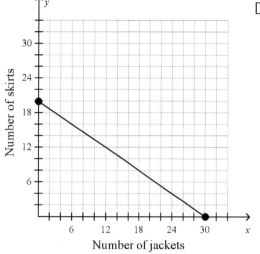

D.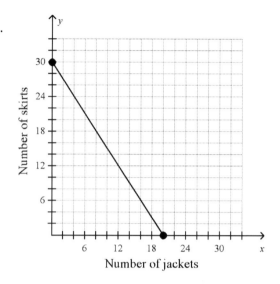

The x-intercept is (0, 20). The x-intercept gives the total number of skirts that can be made from one bolt of fabric when only skirts are made.

The y-intercept is (30, 0). The y-intercept gives the total number of jackets that can be made from one bolt of fabric when only jackets are made.

The x-intercept is (20, 0). The x-intercept gives the total number of jackets that can be made from one bolt of fabric when only jackets are made.

The y-intercept is (0, 30). The y-intercept gives the total number of skirts that can be made from one bolt of fabric when only skirts are made.

Answer Key – Different Forms of Linear Equations

		Marks (C/W)			Marks (C/W)			Marks (C/W)
1	D		31	D		61	B	
2	8		32	A, B, A, A, B		62	A	
3	D		33	C		63	C, E	
4	B		34	A		64	B	
5	C		35	C		65	D	
6	B		36	A		66	B	
7	A		37	B		67	C	
8	C		38	A		68	A	
9	A		39	C		69	D	
10	-6		40	A		70	C	
11	Undefined, C		41	B, A, A, B, B		71	D	
12	A		42	A		72	C	
13	D		43	D		73	Y = 3	
14	A		44	A		74	B	
15	C		45	B		75	A	
16	D		46	C		76	B, D	
17	D		47	A		77	C	
18	B		48	-3		78	C	
19	B, F		49	A, D, E		79	A	
20	Standard Form, $\frac{-1}{2}$		50	C		80	D	
21	C		51	A		81	C	
22	D		52	A, D, F		82	A	
23	A		53	D		83	B, E	
24	A		54	-56		84	B	
25	-2		55	B		85	D	
26	B		56	C		86	A	
27	2.5		57	C		87	B	
28	A		58	C		88	C	
29	A, D		59	B		89	A	
30	C		60	B		90	D	
	Total			Total			Total	

SECTION 4

SYSTEM OF LINEAR EUQATIONS AND INEQUALITY

SYSTEM OF LINEAR EQUATIONS AND INEQUALITY

1. Solve the system of equations given below.

    $2x + 8y = 6$

    $-5x - 20y = -15$

    A. infinitely many solutions
    B. (-8, -16)
    C. no solution
    D. (-4, -8)

2. Solve the system of equations given below.

    $-7x - 8y = 9$

    $-4x + 9y = -22$

    A. no solution
    B. (1, -2)
    C. infinitely many solutions
    D. (-2, 1)

3. The difference of two numbers is 5. Their sum is 17. What is the bigger number?

    Record your answer in the space provided below.

SYSTEM OF LINEAR EQUATIONS AND INEQUALITY

4. Solve the system of equations given by $2x + y = 20$ and $6x - 5y = 12$.

    A. (7, 6)

    B. (-7, -6)

    C. (10, 3.5)

    D. (10, -3.5)

5. Solve the system of equations given below.

    $6x + 2y = -6$

    $7x + 4y = 8$

    A. infinitely many solutions

    B. no solution

    C. (-4, 9)

    D. (4, 8)

6. The sum of two numbers is 36. Twice the first number minus the second is 6. What is difference of these two numbers?

    A. 4

    B. 8

    C. 24

    D. Can't determine

SYSTEM OF LINEAR EQUATIONS AND INEQUALITY

7. Solve the system of equations given below.

   $-5x - 8y = 17$

   $2x - 7y = -17$

   A. (3, 13)
   B. (1, 5)
   C. (-5, 1)
   D. (-8, -16)

8. Which system has no solution?

   A. $\begin{cases} 3y = 3x + 4 \\ y - x = 3 \end{cases}$

   B. $\begin{cases} 2y = 2x + 8 \\ 2x = 2y - 8 \end{cases}$

   C. $\begin{cases} y = \frac{1}{2}x + 6 \\ 2x + 5 = y \end{cases}$

   D. $\begin{cases} y = 4x + 1 \\ y - 1 = 4x \end{cases}$

9. The key club made $238 at their cake sale. They sold rectangle shaped cake for $7 and star shaped cake for $5. They sold twice as many star cakes as rectangle ones, Write the equation below to find how many of each type of cakes did the key club sell?

   Please fill a number in each rectangle box below. Assume 'r' is the number of rectangle cakes they sold and 's' is the number of star shape cakes they sold.

   ☐ r + ☐ s = ☐

   ☐ s = ☐ r

SYSTEM OF LINEAR EQUATIONS AND INEQUALITY

10. Norah and Fatima are selling leather bags for an NGO fund raising. Customers can buy small boxes of leather bags and large boxes of leather bags. Norah sold 3 small boxes of leather bags and 14 large boxes of leather bags for a total of $203. Fatima sold 11 small boxes of leather bags and 11 large boxes of leather bags for a total of $220. Find the cost each of one small box of leather bags and one large box of leather bags.
    A. Small boxes = $6, large boxes of leather bags = $8
    B. Small boxes = $9, large boxes of leather bags = $21
    C. Small boxes = $8, large boxes of leather bags = $15
    D. Small boxes = $7, large boxes of leather bags = $13

11. The cost of renting a ZoomCar for one day includes a flat rental fee plus a charge for each mile the car is driven while it is rented. A ZoomCar that is driven 119 miles costs $108.25. A ZoomCar that is driven 139 miles costs $117.25. What is the flat rental fee?
    A. $19.00
    B. $49.00
    C. $45.60
    D. $54.70

12. Solve the given equations for x and y. $\begin{cases} 3x - y = 14 \\ 2x - y = 10 \end{cases}$

Sign	A. +	B. -

C. 2	D. 3	E. 4	F. 0	G. 5	H. No Solution

X =	AC	AD	AE	BG	BC	BE
Y =	AC	AE	F	BC	BE	BD

Please select one correct answer for each x and y in the grid above.

SYSTEM OF LINEAR EQUATIONS AND INEQUALITY

13. Zahira spent $30.50 on 10 party favors for her party. The party favor for each kid was either a riddle book or a magic painting. The boys each received a riddle book that cost $2.75 each. The girls each received a magic painting that cost $3.25 each. How many boys and how many girls attended the party?
    A. 4 boys and 6 girls
    B. 5 boys and 5 girls
    C. 6 boys and 4 girls
    D. 7 boys and 3 girls

14. The perimeter of a rectangular teak deck is 180 feet. The deck's length, *l*, is 5 feet less than 4 times its width, *w*. Which system of linear equations can be used to determine the dimensions, in feet, of the teak deck?
    A. $2(5w - 5 + w) = 180$
    B. $2(w - 5 + 4w) = 180$
    C. $2(4w - 5 + w) = 180$
    D. $2(4w + 5 - w) = 90$

15. Two snow resorts offer private lessons to their customers. Big Time Ski Mountain charges $10 per hour plus $100 insurance. Powder Hills charges $15 per hour plus $90 insurance. For what number of hours is the cost of lessons the same for each resort?
    Record your answer in the space provided below.

SYSTEM OF LINEAR EQUATIONS AND INEQUALITY

16. Given the system of equations below:

    $3x - 4y = 12$

    $4x - 2y = 11$

    What is the value of y in the solution?

    A. -3.5

    B. 2.5

    C. -1.5

    D. 0.5

17. Solve the give equations for x and y $\begin{cases} 8x - 3y = 13 \\ 3x - 2y = 11 \end{cases}$

    Record your answer in the space provided below.

    ☐

18. A drummer and a guitarist each wrote songs for their band. The guitarist wrote 8 fewer than thrice the number of songs that the drummer wrote. They wrote a total of 56 songs.

    Which system of equations models this situation if the drummer wrote 'd' songs, and the guitarist wrote 'g' songs?

    A. $g = 3d - 8$
    $g + d = 56$

    B. $g = 8 - 3d$
    $g = 56 - d$

    C. $d = 3g - 8$
    $d = 56 - g$

    D. $d = 8 - 3g$
    $d + g = 56$

SYSTEM OF LINEAR EQUATIONS AND INEQUALITY

19. A van travels two different routes: The Yellow Route and the Red Route. The routes are different lengths.
    - On Monday the van traveled the Yellow Route 6 times and the Red Route 5 times, traveling a total of 52 miles.
    - On Tuesday the van traveled the Yellow Route 12 times and the Red Route 13 times, traveling a total of 119 miles.

    What is the length of the Yellow Route in miles?
    A. 4.4 mi
    B. 4.5 mi
    C. 6.4 mi
    D. 6.8 mi

20. What is the value of x in the solution to this system of equations?
    $$y + 2x = -1$$
    $$y = \frac{1}{2}x + 4$$
    A. $\frac{6}{5}$
    B. -2
    C. $-\frac{10}{3}$
    D. 3

SYSTEM OF LINEAR EQUATIONS AND INEQUALITY

21. The graphs of line k_1 and k_2 are shown on the grid.

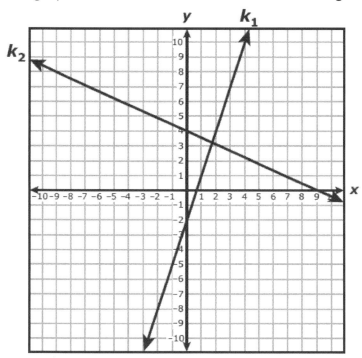

Which system of equation is best represented by this graph?

A. $3x - y = 2$
$4x + 9y = 36$

B. $3x - y = 6$
$4x + 9y = 4$

C. $x - 3y = -18$
$9x + 4y = 9$

D. $x + y = 10$
$9x + 4y = 13$

22. Solve the system of equations given by $x - 4y = 30$ and $3x - 4y = 18$.

   A. (-4, 7)
   B. (-6, -9)
   C. (10, 3.5)
   D. (10, -3.5)

SYSTEM OF LINEAR EQUATIONS AND INEQUALITY

23. Which ordered pair is the solution to the given system of equations?
    y − 2 = 3 (x − 4)
    x − 2y = 5
    A. (3, -1)
    B. (-3, -4)
    C. (9, -3)
    D. (-6, 1)

24. Martin's school is selling tickets to the annual music competition. On the first day of ticket sales the school sold 8 senior citizen tickets and 12 child tickets for a total of $364. The school took in $93 on the second day by selling 1 senior citizen tickets and 4 child tickets. Find the price of a child ticket.
    A. 17
    B. 20
    C. 19
    D. 21

25. Solve the system of equations given by 6x + y = -16 and 12x + 32 = -2y
    A. no solution
    B. infinitely many solutions
    C. (-1, -8)
    D. (1, -2)

SYSTEM OF LINEAR EQUATIONS AND INEQUALITY

26. Solve the system of equations given by 7x + 2y = 28 and 8x + 2y = 32.

Sign		A. +	B. -		
	C. 0	D. 4	E. 6	F. 9	G. 5
X =	AC	AD	AE	BG	BC	BE
Y =	AC	C	F	BC	BE	BD

Please select one correct answer for each x and y in the grid above.

27. Solve the system of equations given below.

    $5x + 2y = -7$

    $-3x - 2y = 1$

    Record your answer in the space below.

28. Solve the system of equations given by 2x + 8y = 6 and x + 4y - 3 = 0

    A. infinitely many solutions
    B. no solution
    C. (5, -1)
    D. (-6, 8)

29. Solve the system of equations given by $\frac{5}{14}x + \frac{2}{7}y + 1 = 0$ and $\frac{1}{2}x + y - 1 = 0$.

    A. (-1, 3)
    B. no solution
    C. (-6, 4)
    D. infinitely many solutions

SYSTEM OF LINEAR EQUATIONS AND INEQUALITY

30. Which statements are true for the system of equations given below. Select all that apply.

    $3x = -15$

    $-y = 11$

    A. Slope for both the lines is 0.
    B. Both the lines are parallel to each other.
    C. Both the lines are perpendicular to each other.
    D. Given lines have exactly one solution.
    E. Line $3x=-15$ is parallel to y-axis.
    F. Line $3x=-15$ is parallel to x-axis.

31. Solve the system of equations given below.

    $4x + 3y = -5$

    $-2x + 2y = 6$

    A. (5, 0)
    B. (0, 9)
    C. (-2, 1)
    D. (3, -4)

32. Solve the system of equations given by $-4x + 2y = 14$ and $4x - 2y = -28$

    A. no solution
    B. many solutions
    C. (-1, -5)
    D. (-2, -8)

33. Complete the statement below for the system of equations given by $3x - 2y = 10$ and $6x - 4y = 20$. Select one correct answer in each box.

    The system of equations has [A. Same / B. Different] slope and [C. Same / D. Different] y-intercept. The given system of equation has [E. One / F. Many / G. None] Solutions.

SYSTEM OF LINEAR EQUATIONS AND INEQUALITY

34. Solve the system of equations given by y = -3 and 2x = -18.

    A. (-9, 0)

    B. (0, -3)

    C. (-9, -3)

    D. No solution

35. Which graph represents the solutions of a - 2 < -4 OR a - 4 > 8?

    A.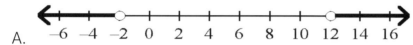

    B.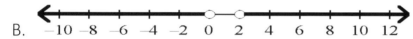

    C.

    D.

36. Graph system of inequality.

    $y \leq -x + 4$
    $y \geq 2x - 3$

    A.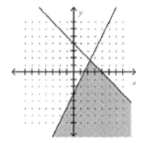
    B.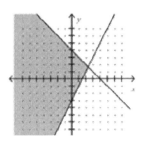
    C.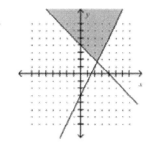
    D.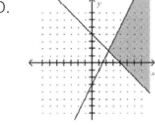

37. Solve for $2x - 6 < -16$ or $2x + 8 > 12$

    A. $x < -5$ or $x > 2$

    B. $x < -5$ or $x > 5$
    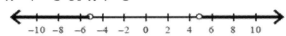

    C. $x < -7$ or $x > 5$
    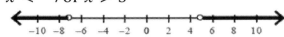

    D. $x < -12$ or > 2
    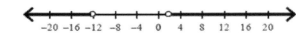

SYSTEM OF LINEAR EQUATIONS AND INEQUALITY

38. Which graph show the solution set of following inequalities.
    $4x - 7 \leq 2x$ and $3x + 5 > -1$?

    A. (number line from -4 to 4)

    B. (number line from -4 to 4)

    C. (number line from -4 to 4)

    D. (number line from -4 to 4)

39. Which graph shows the solution set of the inequalities below.
    $4(3x - 5) < 4(2x - 7)$ and $5x - 10 < 7x$. Select all applicable answers below.

    A. x < -5

    B. x > -5

    C. x > -2

    D. x < -2

    E. x < 2

40. A system of two equations includes one of the equations $y = -\frac{2x}{5} - \frac{1}{2}$. If system has infinitely many solutions, which of the following shows second equation?

    A. $4x + 10y = -5$

    B. $Y + 1 = -\frac{2}{5}\left(x - \frac{5}{4}\right)$

    C. Both A and B

    D. None of above

SYSTEM OF LINEAR EQUATIONS AND INEQUALITY

41. Which statement are true if system of equations has no solution?
    A. Lines have same slope and same y-intercept.
    B. Lines have same slope and different y-intercept.
    C. Lines have different slope and same y-intercept.
    D. Lines have different slope and different y-intercept.
    E. Lines are parallel.

42. Which statement are true if system of equations has one solution?
    A. Lines have same slope and same y-intercept.
    B. Lines have same slope and different y-intercept.
    C. Lines have different slope and same y-intercept.
    D. Lines have different slope and different y-intercept.

43. Which inequality is represented by the graph below?

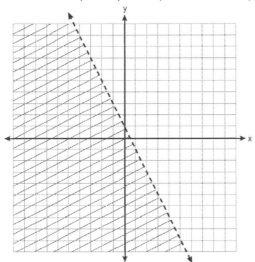

A. $y < 2x + 1$
B. $y < -2x + 1$
C. $y < \frac{1}{2}x + 1$
D. $y < -\frac{1}{2}x + 1$

SYSTEM OF LINEAR EQUATIONS AND INEQUALITY

44. Which inequality is shown on the graph below?

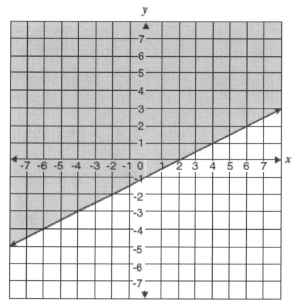

A. $y < \frac{1}{2}x - 1$

B. $y \leq \frac{1}{2}x - 1$

C. $y > \frac{1}{2}x - 1$

D. $y \geq \frac{1}{2}x - 1$

45. Which graph best represents $2x - y < 10$?

A.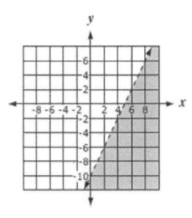

B.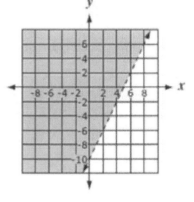

C.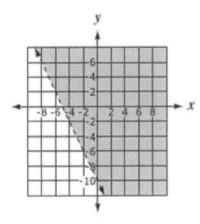

D.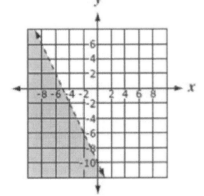

46. Which is a graph of the solution set of the inequality $3x - 4y \leq 24$?

A.
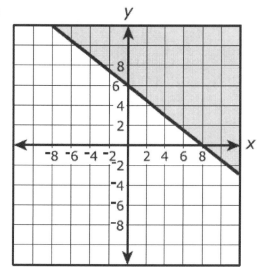

B.
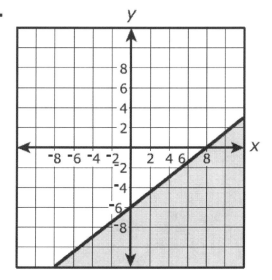

C.
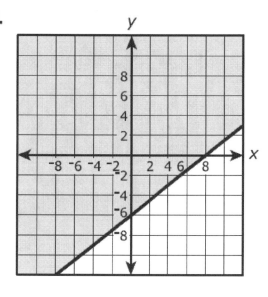

D.
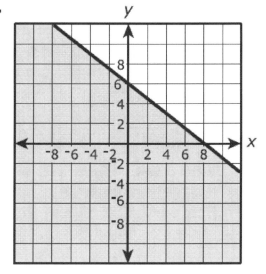

47. Which graph best represents the solution set of $y \leq -4x$?

A.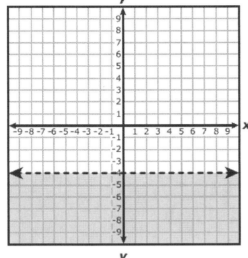
B.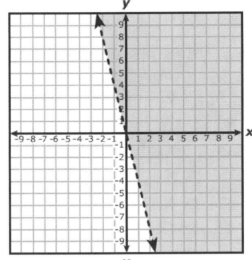
C.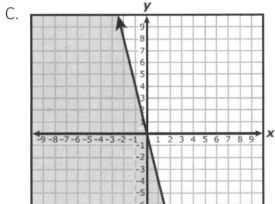
D.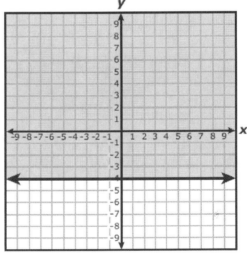

48. Which of the system of inequality is shown for graph below assuming slope of solid line is 1?

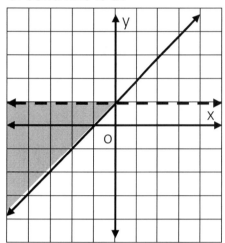

A. $x < 1$ and $y \geq x + 1$
B. $y \leq 1$ and $x - y < 1$
C. $y < 1$ and $y - x > 1$
D. $y < 1$ and $y - x \geq 1$

SYSTEM OF LINEAR EQUATIONS AND INEQUALITY

49. Which of the inequality does not belong to graph below?

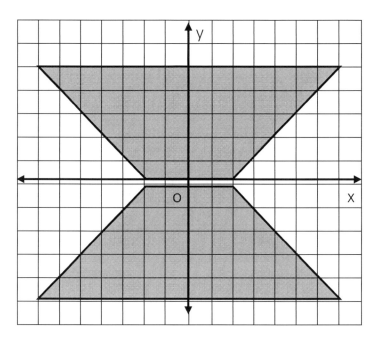

A. $y \geq -x + 2$
B. $y \leq -x + 2$
C. $y \geq x - 2$
D. $y \geq 5$

SYSTEM OF LINEAR EQUATIONS AND INEQUALITY

50. Which of the inequality does not belong to graph below?

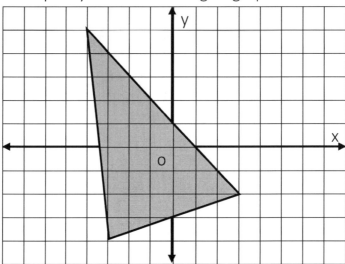

A. $y \leq -x + 1$
B. $y \geq \frac{1}{3}x - 3$
C. $y \geq -9x - 31$
D. $y \leq x + 1$

51. Which equation represents 'Line 1' graphed below?

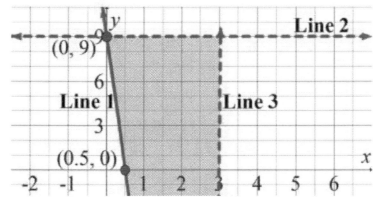

A. $y \leq 9x + 9$
B. $y \geq 9x + 9$
C. $y \leq -18x + 9$
D. $y \geq -18x + 9$

SYSTEM OF LINEAR EQUATIONS AND INEQUALITY

52. Harry's $2,200 savings is in two accounts 'A' and 'B'. Account 'A' earns 2% annual interest, and the account 'B' earns 4%. His total interest for the year is $69. Which equation can represent the scenario if x is the amount invested in account A and y is the amount invested in account B?

    A. x + y = 1100
        2x + 4y = 69
    B. x + y = 2200
        0.02x + 0.04y = 138
    C. x + y = 2200
        0.02x + 0.04y = 69
    D. x + y = 2200
        2x + 4y = 138

53. A $5,200 principal is invested in two accounts, one earning 3% interest and another earning 6% interest. If the total interest for the year is $210, then how much is invested in account which earns 6%? Record your answer in the space provided below.

    [   ]

54. A jar consisting of only dimes and quarters contains 70 coins. Which system of equation can be used to find number of dimes and quarters if total value of coins is $9.10? 'Q' shows number of quarters and 'N' shows number of dimes.

    A. Q + D = 70
        25Q + 5D = 9.10
    B. Q + D = 910
        25Q + 10D = 70
    C. Q + D = 70
        0.25Q + 0.10D = 910
    D. Q + D = 70
        25Q + 10D = 910

SYSTEM OF LINEAR EQUATIONS AND INEQUALITY

55. Jill has $9.20 worth of dimes and quarters. If there are 68 coins in total, how many of dimes does she have?

Answer Key – System of Linear Equations and Inequality

		Marks (C/W)			Marks (C/W)
1	A		31	C	
2	B		32	A	
3	11		33	A, C, F	
4	A		34	C	
5	C		35	A	
6	B		36	B	
7	C		37	A	
8	A		38	D	
9	$7r + 5s = 238$, $s = 2r$		39	B, D	
10	D		40	C	
11	D		41	B, E	
12	AE, BC		42	C, D	
13	A		43	B	
14	C		44	D	
15	2		45	B	
16	C		46	C	
17	(-1,-7)		47	C	
18	A		48	D	
19	B		49	D	
20	B		50	D	
21	A		51	D	
22	B		52	C	
23	A		53	$1800	
24	C		54	D	
25	B		55	52	
26	AD, C				
27	(-3, 4)				
28	A				
29	C				
30	C, D, E				
	Total			Total	

SECTION 5

RADICALS, EXPONENTS AND EXPONENTIAL FUNCTIONS

RADICALS, EXPONENTS AND EXPONENTIAL FUNCTIONS

1. What are the missing exponent and coefficient in the equation below? Give the missing exponent first.

$$2(3m^5)^? = ?\, m^{-10}$$

   A. -5; -30
   B. -2; -18
   C. -2; $\frac{2}{9}$
   D. -2; -$\frac{2}{9}$

2. What are the missing exponents in the equation below? Give the missing exponent on the left side first.

   $3(m^7 n)^? = 3m^? n^4$

   A. 4; 11
   B. 3; 12
   C. 3; 28
   D. 4; 28

3. Adam needs to simplify the expression below before he substitutes values for a and b.

   $$\frac{a^{15}b^{12} - a^5 b^8}{a^3 b^2}$$

   If $a \neq 0$ and $b \neq 0$, which of the following is an equivalent expression for above?

   A. $a^5 b^6 - a^5 b^4$
   B. $a^{12} b^{10} - a^2 b^6$
   C. $a^6 b^4$
   D. $a^7 b^2$

RADICALS, EXPONENTS AND EXPONENTIAL FUNCTIONS

4. Simplify $(4a^3b^{-2})^{-3}$

   A. $\dfrac{b^6}{64a^9}$

   B. $\dfrac{64b^6}{a^9}$

   C. $-64a^{-9}b^6$

   D. $\dfrac{-12a^{-6}}{b^5}$

5. Which equation represents exponential decay? Select one correct answer in each box to complete the sentence.

   $$y = 1.05(0.65)^x$$

   Given function represents exponential
   - A. Growth
   - B. Decay

   at a rate of
   - C. 105 %
   - D. 65 %
   - E. 35 %

   with initial value
   - F. 0.15
   - G. 1.05
   - H. 0.65

6. Given the coordinates (0, 3), (1, 11), (2, 19), (3, 27), would a graph of these points exhibit exponential behavior?

   A. no, it would not display exponential or linear behavior

   B. yes, exponential behavior only

   C. yes, exponential *and* linear behavior

   D. no, it would display linear behavior

RADICALS, EXPONENTS AND EXPONENTIAL FUNCTIONS

7. For equations of the form $y = b^x$, where b is a constant, what is true about b if the y-values change little for small values of x, but increase quickly for large x values?

    A. $b = 1$

    B. $0 < b < 1$

    C. $b > 1$

    D. $-1 < b < 0$

8. Suppose Chang sprayed around the house for ants. Which formula would be used to find the number of ants still alive after a certain time if the number of ants was changing exponentially?

    A. exponential growth

    B. cannot be determined from given information

    C. exponential decay

    D. compound interest

9. $3^{1.5}$ can also be written as

    A. 4.5

    B. $3\sqrt{3}$

    C. 0.5

    D. 6

RADICALS, EXPONENTS AND EXPONENTIAL FUNCTIONS

10. What is the y-intercept of the graph of $y = 4^{x-2}$? Record your answer in the space provided below.

11. What are the missing number and exponent in the equation below?
    $(-2m^7n)^{-3} = ?m^?n^{-3}$
    A. 8; 10
    B. -8; 4
    C. $\frac{-1}{8}$; -21
    D. -6; 21

12. Simplify $(-2^2x^2y^3)(-x^4y^4)$. Select one correct answer from each box below to complete the sentence.

    Leading coefficient is [○ -2 / ○ -4 / ○ 4], exponent value on variable x [○ 2 / ○ 4 / ○ 6]

    and exponent value on variable y is [○ 7 / ○ 12 / ○ 6]

13. The area of a parallelogram is $54p^6q^6$ square units. If the base of the parallelogram measures $6pq^2$ units, what is the height of the parallelogram? $(p > 0$ and $q > 0)$
    A. $9p^5q^4$ units
    B. $9p^6q^3$ units
    C. $48p^5q^4$ units
    D. $48p^6q^3$ units

RADICALS, EXPONENTS AND EXPONENTIAL FUNCTIONS

14. The side length of a square is $6x^3yz^4$ units. What is the area of the square?

   A. $12x^6y^2z^8$ square units
   B. $12x^9yz^{16}$ square units
   C. $36x^6y^2z^8$ square units
   D. $36x^9yz^{16}$ square units

15. Which expression represents $\frac{(3x^2)(8x^6)}{4x^6}$ in simplest form?

   A. $6x^2$
   B. $6x^9$
   C. $4x^2$
   D. $4x^9$

16. Which expression is equivalent to $x^6 x^2$?

   A. $x^4 x^3$
   B. $x^5 x^3$
   C. $x^7 x^3$
   D. $x^9 x^3$

17. Simplify $\frac{4x^{-2}y}{3y^{-3}}$

   Record your answer in the space provided below.

RADICALS, EXPONENTS AND EXPONENTIAL FUNCTIONS

18. Simplify $(x^6)^3$.

    A. x^2

    B. x^3

    C. x^9

    D. x^{18}

19. Which of the following expressions are equal to 1? Assume variables represent positive numbers. Select all applicable answers.

    A. $3x^0$

    B. $10(x^0)$

    C. x^1

    D. $(2x)^0$

    E. $(4x+3)°$

20. Pierre needs to simplify the expression below before he substitutes values for x and y.

    $$\frac{x^{16}y^8 + x^6y^2}{x^2y^2}$$

    If x ≠ 0 and y ≠ 0, which of the following is an equivalent expression for above?

    A. $x^{14}y^6 + x^4y^2$

    B. $x^{14}y^6 + x^4$

    C. $x^{11}y^5$

    D. $x^{20}y^9$

RADICALS, EXPONENTS AND EXPONENTIAL FUNCTIONS

21. What are the missing exponent and coefficient in the equation below? Give the missing exponent first.

    $3(2m^{-5})^? = ?\, m^{-10}$

    A. -5; 6
    B. -2; -18
    C. 12; 2
    D. 2; 12

22. Divide. Simplify your answer.

    $(12x^4 - 18x^3 + 36x^2) \div (6x^3)$

    A. $12x - 18 + \frac{36}{x}$
    B. $2x - 3 + \frac{6}{x}$
    C. $2x^4 - 3x^3 + 6x^2$
    D. $6x - \frac{12}{x^2} + \frac{30}{x^3}$

23. Simplify the following expression

    $$\frac{(2x^{16}y^9)x^6y^2}{4x^2y^2}$$

    A. $2x^{20}y^9$
    B. $0.5x^{20}y^9$
    C. $2x^{11}y^9$
    D. $x^{11}y^9$

RADICALS, EXPONENTS AND EXPONENTIAL FUNCTIONS

24. Divide $(8y^4 - 8y^2 + 2)$ by $4y^3$.

   A. $\dfrac{2}{y} + \dfrac{1}{2y^3}$

   B. $\dfrac{2}{y} - 2y + 2y^3$

   C. $2y - \dfrac{2}{y} + \dfrac{1}{2y^3}$

   D. $2y - 8y^2 + 2$

25. Write the expression $\sqrt[3]{8a^2} \cdot \sqrt[3]{8ab^5}$ in exponential form.

   A. $8^{\frac{1}{3}}ab^2$

   B. $8^{\frac{2}{3}}a^{\frac{1}{3}}b^{\frac{5}{3}}$

   C. $4ab^{\frac{5}{3}}$

   D. $64a^3b^5$

26. Simplify the expression
   $\left(3a^{\frac{1}{5}} \cdot t^{\frac{2}{7}}\right)\left(2a^{\frac{4}{5}} \cdot t^{\frac{4}{7}}\right)$

   A. $6at^2$

   B. $6at$

   C. $6at^{\frac{6}{7}}$

   D. $6a^{\frac{4}{5}}t^{\frac{8}{7}}$

RADICALS, EXPONENTS AND EXPONENTIAL FUNCTIONS

27. Simplify $(7a^4b)(8a^7b^6)$.

   A. $56a^{28}b^6$

   B. $56a^{11}b^7$

   C. $15a^{28}b^6$

   D. $15a^{11}b^6$

28. Simplify $(4x^2y)(2xy^2z^3)^3$. Record your answer in the space provided below.

29. The area of the rectangle shown below is $4x^3y^2$, and its base b is $2x^5y$. Find the height, h.

   A. $2x^2y$

   B. $8x^8y^3$

   C. $\dfrac{2x}{y^2}$

   D. $\dfrac{2y}{x^2}$

RADICALS, EXPONENTS AND EXPONENTIAL FUNCTIONS

30. Find the volume of the rectangular solid shown below.

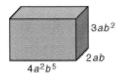

   A. $24a^2b^7$
   B. $24a^2b^{10}$
   C. $24a^4b^8$
   D. $9a^4b^8$

31. Simplify $(4y^4)^3$.
   A. $64y^{12}$
   B. $64y^{64}$
   C. $12y^3$
   D. $12y^{12}$

32. Simplify $(3a^4b^5c)^4$.
   A. $7a^{16}b^{20}c^4$
   B. $81a^{16}b^{20}c^4$
   C. $12a^8b^9c^5$
   D. $3a^{16}b^{20}c^4$

RADICALS, EXPONENTS AND EXPONENTIAL FUNCTIONS

33. The sequence below is:

    -1, -2, -6, -24, -120

    A. Arithmetic

    B. Geometric

    C. Quadratic

    D. None of above

34. Which expression is NOT equivalent to the other expressions?

    A. $(4x^2y)^2$

    B. $4x^4y^2$

    C. $16x^4y^2$

    D. $4^2x^4y^2$

35. A geometric sequence has a common ratio of -4. The 5th term is 2. Find its 2nd term? Record your answer in the space below.

36. Simplify the expression $\sqrt{\dfrac{48}{196}}$.

    A. $\dfrac{4}{7}$

    B. $\dfrac{2}{7}\sqrt{3}$

    C. $\dfrac{16}{49}$

    D. $\dfrac{\sqrt{48}}{\sqrt{196}}$

RADICALS, EXPONENTS AND EXPONENTIAL FUNCTIONS

37. Simplify the expression $\dfrac{\sqrt{15}}{\sqrt{2}}$.

    A. $\dfrac{\sqrt{15}}{2}$

    B. $\dfrac{\sqrt{30}}{2}$

    C. $\sqrt{7.5}$

    D. $\dfrac{2}{\sqrt{30}}$

38. Multiply. Write the product in simplest form.

    $$\sqrt{6}(\sqrt{4}+\sqrt{6})$$

    A. $\sqrt{24}+\sqrt{36}$

    B. $2\sqrt{6}+6$

    C. $12+6\sqrt{6}$

    D. $2\sqrt{15}$

39. Kush simplified the expression below on the class.

    $$\sqrt{20}+\sqrt{5x}+3\sqrt{5}$$

    If Kush simplified the expression correctly, which of the following is his answer?

    A. $5\sqrt{5}+\sqrt{5x}$

    B. $7\sqrt{5}+\sqrt{5x}$

    C. $3\sqrt{5}+\sqrt{5x}$

    D. $4\sqrt{5}+\sqrt{5x}$

RADICALS, EXPONENTS AND EXPONENTIAL FUNCTIONS

40. Simplify below in form of ab.

    $2\sqrt{605} \cdot \sqrt{55}$

    Select one answer from each box below.

    a =
    A. 18
    B. 110
    C. 115
    D. 65

    b =
    A. $\sqrt{5}$
    B. $\sqrt{11}$
    C. $\sqrt{55}$

41. Simplify.

    $$\frac{\sqrt{1050}}{\sqrt{1470}}$$

    A. $\frac{\sqrt{35}}{7}$

    B. $\frac{5\sqrt{6}}{\sqrt{30}}$

    C. $\frac{30\sqrt{35}}{7}$

    D. $\frac{5\sqrt{42}}{7\sqrt{30}}$

42. What is the simplest form of the expression below?

    $4\sqrt{2} + 3\sqrt{2} - 5\sqrt{2}$

    A. $2\sqrt{2}$
    B. $2\sqrt{6}$
    C. $7\sqrt{2}$
    D. $12\sqrt{2}$

RADICALS, EXPONENTS AND EXPONENTIAL FUNCTIONS

43. The pressure exerted on the floor by a person's shoe heel depends on the weight of the person and the width of the heel. The formula is
$$P = \frac{1.2w}{H^2},$$
Where P is pressure in pounds per square inch, W is weight in pounds, and H is heel width in inches. Which of the following shows the pressure formula solved for H?

   A. $H = \pm\sqrt{1.2WP}$

   B. $H = \pm\sqrt{\frac{1.2W}{P}}$

   C. $H = \pm\frac{1.2W}{P}$

   D. $H = \frac{1.2W}{2P}$

44. Rafael knows the height and the required volume of a cone-shaped vase he is designing. Which formula can he use to determine the radius of the vase if $V = \frac{\pi r^2 h}{3}$? Select the correct answer.

   A. $r = \sqrt{\frac{V}{3\pi h}}$

   B. $r = \sqrt{\frac{3V}{\pi h}}$

   C. $r = \sqrt{\frac{9V}{\pi h}}$

   D. $r = \pm\sqrt{\frac{3V}{\pi h}}$

RADICALS, EXPONENTS AND EXPONENTIAL FUNCTIONS

45. A 30-foot pole is stabilized by a wire attached to the ground 10 feet from the base of the pole. How long is the wire? Give your answer as a radical expression in simplest form.

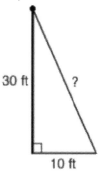

A. $2\sqrt{5}$ ft
B. $2\sqrt{10}$ ft
C. $10\sqrt{10}$ ft
D. $20\sqrt{2}$ ft

46. Simplify $\sqrt{\frac{300}{49}}$.

A. $\frac{3\sqrt{10}}{7}$
B. $\frac{3}{7}$
C. $\frac{10\sqrt{3}}{7}$
D. $\frac{30}{7}$

RADICALS, EXPONENTS AND EXPONENTIAL FUNCTIONS

47. Which expression is equivalent to $\sqrt{147}$?

    A. $3\sqrt{7}$

    B. $7\sqrt{3}$

    C. $21\sqrt{7}$

    D. $49\sqrt{3}$

48. Add $\sqrt{27} + \sqrt{48} + \sqrt{75}$.

    A. Cannot combine

    B. $5\sqrt{6}$

    C. $12\sqrt{3}$

    D. $50\sqrt{3}$

49. Multiply. Write the product in simplest form.

    $\sqrt{2}(\sqrt{2} + \sqrt{5})$

    A. $2 + \sqrt{10}$

    B. $\sqrt{4} + \sqrt{10}$

    C. $\sqrt{14}$

    D. $2\sqrt{2} + 2\sqrt{5}$

RADICALS, EXPONENTS AND EXPONENTIAL FUNCTIONS

50. Suppose that we have a 3 ft. × 3 ft. piece of paper, and we cut out a square piece so that the area of the remaining piece is 5 feet. What is the length of a side of the square?

    A. 2 ft.

    B. $\sqrt{2}$

    C. $\sqrt{5}$

    D. 4 ft.

51. Select one correct answer from each box below to complete the sentence.

    The given geometric sequence 4, 10, 25... has ratio of

    | A. 2.5 |
    | B. 0.4 |

    and the next 3 terms are ...., ..., ...

52. Select one correct answer from each box below to complete the sentence.

    The geometric sequence 4, 28, 196,.... has ratio of

    | A. 7 |
    | B. $\frac{1}{7}$ |
    | C. 24 |

    and the 6th term is ....

53. Sameera invested $1000 in an account at 8% interest compounded yearly. How much money will she have earned on the account after 7 years?

    A. $1,713.82

    B. $1,741.02

    C. $713.82

    D. $741.02

RADICALS, EXPONENTS AND EXPONENTIAL FUNCTIONS

54. Determine whether the sequence 3, 12, 48, 192 is geometric. If so, find its common ratio.
    A. geometric, $r = 4$
    B. geometric, $r = 3$
    C. not geometric
    D. geometric, $r = 9$

55. A formula in which the nth term of a sequence is expressed in terms of the previous term, as in is called what?
    A. Exponential
    B. Geometric
    C. Recursive
    D. Explicit

56. Nancy invests $100 in one account for ten years at 9% interest rate compounded annually. How much interest will she earn in 10 years? Round your answer to the nearest tenth.
    A. $237.70
    B. $136.70
    C. $108.20
    D. $1090

RADICALS, EXPONENTS AND EXPONENTIAL FUNCTIONS

57. Each year, new computers are built with better technology, making older ones less valuable. If the computers lose value at a rate of 20% per year, how much will a $1500 computer be worth in ten years?

   A. $1,200
   B. $161.06
   C. $9,287.60
   D. near $0

58. What is the eighth term of the geometric sequence whose first three terms are 3, 6, and 12?

   A. 768
   B. 128
   C. 256
   D. 384

59. Given the explicit formula for a geometric sequence, find the initial value and 8th term.

   $f(n) = -2.5(4)^{n-1}$

   Select one correct answer from each box below to complete the sentence.

   Initial value is [A. 2.5 B. 1 C. -2.5] and 8th term is [D. -40,960 E. 16,384 F. 40,960 G. -16384]

60. $50,000 is invested at 5.5% compounded annually. How much will be in the account after 5 years.

   A. $68,257
   B. $65,348
   C. $69,456
   D. $63,634

RADICALS, EXPONENTS AND EXPONENTIAL FUNCTIONS

61. In 2010, the number of students in a small school is 435. It is estimated that the number of students will increase at a rate of 3% per year. Which formula will be helpful to find number of student's 'N' in 2019?
    A. $N = 435(3)^{2019}$
    B. $N = 435(3)^9$
    C. $N = 435(0.03)^{2019}$
    D. $N = 435(1 + 0.03)^9$

62. If $2^x = 16$, find the value of 2^{x+4}.
    A. 216
    B. 256
    C. 729
    D. 324

63. Find the perimeter of the following figure.

    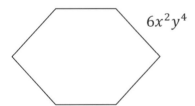

    A. $7776x^2y^4$
    B. $36x^2y^4$
    C. $30x^{12}y^{24}$
    D. $6x^{12}y^{24}$

RADICALS, EXPONENTS AND EXPONENTIAL FUNCTIONS

64. What is the area of the rectangle with the width of $6x^2$ and the length of $12x^3$.
    A. $72x^5$
    B. $18x^5$
    C. $6x^5$
    D. $72x^6$

65. What is the area of a square with the length of a side equaling $3a^5$?
    A. $6a^4$
    B. $9a^5$
    C. $9a^{10}$
    D. $12a^5$

66. Simon plays basketball for his school. He scored 14 points on Monday, and he doubled his score each day thereafter. How many points did he score on Thursday?
    A. 224 points
    B. 112 points
    C. 56 points
    D. 42 points

67. Suppose a population of 250 crickets doubles in size every 6 months. How many crickets will there be after 2 years?
    A. 4,000 crickets
    B. 6,000 crickets
    C. 2,000 crickets
    D. 1,000 crickets

RADICALS, EXPONENTS AND EXPONENTIAL FUNCTIONS

68. Review the graph and select one correct answer from each box below.

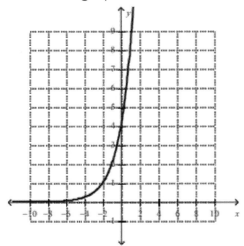

The graph is defined by function f(x)=

A. $y = 4(2^x)$
B. $y = 10(4^x)$
C. $y = 4(0.75^x)$
D. $y = -3(-2^x)$

and has domain as

E. All real numbers
F. X > 0
G. X < 0

69. Which is an example of exponential function?
   A. $f(x) = 5x^2$
   B. $f(x) = x^5$
   C. $f(x) = 5^x$
   D. Both A and B

70. Find common ratio for function given below.

n	1	2	3	4	5
f(n)	$\frac{1}{3}$	$\frac{2}{9}$	$\frac{4}{27}$	$\frac{8}{81}$	$\frac{16}{243}$

   A. $\frac{1}{3}$
   B. $\frac{2}{3}$
   C. 3
   D. None of the above

RADICALS, EXPONENTS AND EXPONENTIAL FUNCTIONS

71. The half-life of Cobalt-60 is 5 years. If Dr. Richard has 10 grams of Co-60, how much will he have after 15 years? Half-life formula is given by $N = N_0(\frac{1}{2})^{\frac{t}{h}}$, where 't' is time and 'h' is half-life of the object/element.

    A. 0.5 grams
    B. 10 grams
    C. 1.5 grams
    D. 1.25 grams

72. Which exponential function describes the sequence of numbers?
$$3, \frac{3}{2}, \frac{3}{4}, \frac{3}{8}, \ldots$$

    A. $y = \frac{1}{2} \cdot 3^x$
    B. $y = 6 \cdot \left(\frac{1}{2}\right)^x$
    C. $y = 3 + \left(\frac{1}{2}\right)^x$
    D. $y = \left(\frac{1}{2}\right)^x - 3$

73. Which of the following functions describe exponential growth? Select all applicable answers.

    A. $y = 4(1 + 0.03)^x$
    B. $y = y = 4(0.3)^x$
    C. y = 0.1(2)x
    D. $y = (1.01)^x$
    E. $y = \frac{3}{4}(5)^{x-1}$

RADICALS, EXPONENTS AND EXPONENTIAL FUNCTIONS

74. For equations of the form $y = a^x$, where a is a constant, what is true about 'a' if the y-values remains same as x-values?

A. $a = 1$

B. $0 < a < 1$

C. $a > 1$

D. $-1 < a < 0$

75. Which is the graph of $y = 2.5^x$?

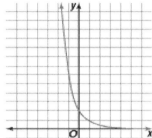
A.

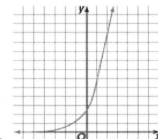
C.

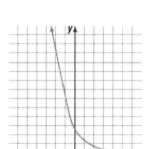
B.

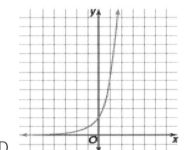
D.

RADICALS, EXPONENTS AND EXPONENTIAL FUNCTIONS

76. What is the function rule that describes the graph?

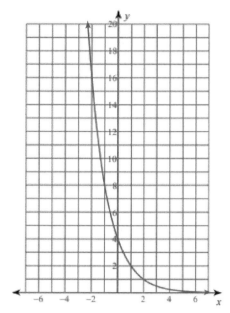

A. $y = 4 \cdot 2^x$

B. $y = 4 \cdot \left(\frac{1}{2}\right)^x$

C. $y = 2 \cdot \left(\frac{1}{2}\right)^x$

D. $y = 5 \cdot 2^x$

77. Which exponential function describes the sequence of numbers?

   1, 2, 4, 8, 16

A. $2^{(x-1)}$

B. $4^{(x-1)}$

C. $3^{(x-1)}$

D. $6^{(x-1)}$

RADICALS, EXPONENTS AND EXPONENTIAL FUNCTIONS

78. Which of the following function describe exponential decay?

    A. 9^x

    B. $y = \left(\dfrac{1}{5}\right)^x$

    C. $y = 4^x$

    D. $y = \left(\dfrac{12}{7}\right)^x$

79. Which of the following function describe exponential growth?

    A. 1.9^x

    B. $y = \left(\dfrac{1}{5}\right)^x$

    C. $2\left(\dfrac{1}{2}\right)^x$

    D. $y = \left(\dfrac{5}{6}\right)^x$

80. Which exponential function describes following sequence?

    $$5, 15, 45, 135, 405, 1215$$

    A. $y = 4(2)^x$
    B. $y = 2(3)^x$
    C. $y = 5(2)^x$
    D. $y = 5(3)^x$

RADICALS, EXPONENTS AND EXPONENTIAL FUNCTIONS

Answer Key – Radicals, Exponents and Exponential Functions

		Marks (C/W)			Marks (C/W)			Marks (C/W)
1	C		31	A		61	D	
2	D		32	B		62	B	
3	B		33	D		63	B	
4	A		34	B		64	A	
5	B, E, G		35	$\frac{-1}{32}$		65	C	
6	D		36	B		66	B	
7	C		37	B		67	A	
8	C		38	B		68	A, E	
9	B		39	A		69	C	
10	$\frac{1}{16}$		40	B, B		70	B	
11	C		41	A		71	D	
12	4, 6, 7		42	A		72	B	
13	A		43	B		73	A, D, E	
14	C		44	B		74	A	
15	A		45	C		75	D	
16	B		46	C		76	B	
17	$\frac{4y^4}{3x^2}$		47	B		77	A	
18	D		48	C		78	B	
19	D, E		49	A		79	A	
20	B		50	A		80	D	
21	D		51	2.5, 62.5, 156.25, 390.625				
22	B		52	7, 67228				
23	B		53	A				
24	C		54	A				
25	C		55	C				
26	C		56	B				
27	B		57	B				
28	$32x^5y^7z^9$		58	D				
29	D		59	C, F				
30	C		60	B				
	Total			Total			Total	

SECTION 6

POLYNOMIAL FUNCTIONS

POLYNOMIAL FUNCTIONS

1. What is the degree of $4x^3 - 5xy^4 + 3xy^2 - 1$?
   A. 0
   B. 5
   C. 3
   D. 4

2. Find the sum $(4xy^2 - 3x^2y - 5xy - 6) + (-5xy^2 - 2xy + 3)$.
   A. $4xy^2 - 8x^2y - 7xy - 3$
   B. $-xy^2 - 3x^2y - 7xy - 3$
   C. $-xy^2 - 3x^2y - 3xy - 3$
   D. $4xy^2 - 7xy - 3$

3. Solve $4a(a - 4) - 27a = a(4a - 3) + 20$.
   A. $a = -\dfrac{1}{2}$
   B. $a = -2$
   C. $a = -\dfrac{3}{2}$
   D. $a = -\dfrac{3}{4}$

4. Find $(5t^2 - 2w)^2$
   A. $25t^4 - 4w^2$
   B. $25t^4 + 4w^2$
   C. $25t^4 - 10t^2w + 4w^2$
   D. $25t^4 - 20t^2w + 4w^2$

POLYNOMIAL FUNCTIONS

5. Write a polynomial to represent the area of a square with a side x minus the area of a triangle with a base $2x$ and a height of 5.
   A. $4x$
   B. $x^2 - 5x$
   C. $x^2 - 10x$
   D. $x^2 - 2x + 5$

6. George and Nadal each throw a football. The height of George's throw can represent by the equation $A = -11x^2 + 19x + 27$, where A is height and x is the time in seconds. The height of Nadal's throw can represent by the equation $S = -10x^2 + 10x + 18$. At time x, what is the combined height of the throws?
   A. $-x^2 + x - 1$
   B. $-21x^2 + 29x + 45$
   C. $x^2 - x + 1$
   D. $21x^2 + 29x + 45$

7. Multiply $4x^2 (-x^2 - 4x + 3)$.
   A. $-4x^4 - 16x^3 + 12x^2$
   B. $-4x^4 - 8x^3 + 12x^2$
   C. $-4x^2 - 16x + 12$
   D. $-4x^2 - 8x + 12$

POLYNOMIAL FUNCTIONS

8. Find the product $(2x - 3)(2x^2 + 5x - 1)$.
    A. $8x^2 - 17x - 3$
    B. $4x^3 + 4x^2 - 17x - 3$
    C. $8x^2 - 17x + 3$
    D. $4x^3 + 4x^2 - 17x + 3$

9. Find the product $(x^2 - 3x + 6)(2x^2 + 3x + 4)$.
    A. $2x^4 - 3x^3 + 7x^2 + 6x + 24$
    B. $2x^4 + 3x^3 + 7x^2 + 6x + 24$
    C. $2x^4 + 3x^3 - 5x^2 + 6x + 24$
    D. $2x^4 - 3x^3 - 5x^2 + 6x + 24$

10. Which of the following is a difference of two squares?
    A. $x^2 - 9$
    B. $x^2 - 8x - 16$
    C. $x^2 + 36$
    D. $x^2 + 6x + 9$

11. Write $6x^4y^2 - 4x^2y + 2xy^3 + 8$ in standard form.
    A. $8 - 4x^2y + 6x^4y^2 + 2xy^3$
    B. $8 + 2xy^3 - 4x^2y + 6x^4y^2$
    C. $2xy^3 + 6x^4y^2 - 4x^2y + 8$
    D. $6x^4y^2 + 2xy^3 - 4x^2y + 8$

POLYNOMIAL FUNCTIONS

12. Simplify $5a(4a^2 - 2a) + 3a(-2a^2 + 4a)$.
    A. $14a^2 + 2a$
    B. $2a^2 + 10a$
    C. $10a^3 + 4a^2$
    D. $14a^3 + 2a^2$

13. Find $(x - 4)^2$.
    A. $x^2 - 16$
    B. $x^2 + 16$
    C. $x^2 - 8x + 16$
    D. $x^2 - 4x + 16$

14. Find $(3a + 4b)^2$
    A. $9a^2 + 16b^2$
    B. $9a^2 + 24ab + 16b^2$
    C. $3a^2 + 24ab + 4b^2$
    D. $9a^2 + 12ab + 16b^2$

15. Write an expression for the area of the rectangle.

    (Rectangle with width $x + 8$ and length $x^2 - 4x + 5$)

    A. $x^3 - 4x$
    B. $9x^2 - 31x + 40$
    C. $x^2 - 3x + 13$
    D. $x^3 + 4x^2 - 27x + 40$

POLYNOMIAL FUNCTIONS

16. Anthony and Sanford each throw a football. The height of Anthony's throw can be represented by the equation $A = -10x^2 + 15x + 22$, where A is height and x is the time in seconds. The height of Sanford's throw can be represented by the equation $S = -9x^2 + 14x + 23$. At time x, how much higher is Sanford's throw?

    A. $x^2 + x + 1$
    B. $x^2 + x - 1$
    C. $x^2 - x + 1$
    D. $x^2 - x - 1$

17. The measures of two sides of a triangle are given. If P is the perimeter, and $P = 18x + 9y$, find the measure of the third side.

    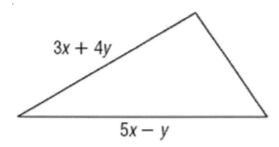

    A. 10x + 12y
    B. 26x + 12y
    C. 10x + 6y
    D. 28x − 6y

18. A rectangle has a base of 5x − 1 and a height of 4x + 2. What is the area?
    A. $20x^2 - 6x - 2$
    B. $20x^2 - 6x + 2$
    C. $20x^2 + 6x + 2$
    D. $20x^2 + 6x - 2$

POLYNOMIAL FUNCTIONS

19. What is the degree of $16x^5 - 8pxy^4 + 4xy^2 - 2p$?
    A. 4
    B. 6
    C. 5
    D. 3

20. Find the sum $(4xy^2 - 3x^2y - 5xy - 6) + (-5xy^2 - 2xy + 3)$.
    A. $4xy^2 - 7xy - 3$
    B. $-xy^2 - 3x^2y - 7xy - 3$
    C. $-xy^2 - 3x^2y - 3xy - 3$
    D. $4xy^2 - 8x^2y - 7xy - 3$

21. Find $-8x^3y^2(3xy^4 - 2x^5 - y)$.
    A. $-24x^4y^6 + 16x^8y^2 + 8x^3y^3$
    B. $-5x^4y^6 - 10x^8y^2 - 9x^3y^3$
    C. $-24x^4y^6 + 16x^{15}y^2 + 8x^3y^3$
    D. $-24x^4y^6 - 16x^8y^2 + 8x^3y^3$

22. Simplify $5a(4a^2 - 2a) + 3a(-2a^2 + 4a)$.
    A. $2a^2 + 10a$
    B. $14a^3 + 2a^2$
    C. $10a^3 + 4a^2$
    D. $14a^2 + 2a$

POLYNOMIAL FUNCTIONS

23. Find $(x-6)^2$.
    A. $x^2 + 36$
    B. $x^2 - 12x + 36$
    C. $x^2 - 8x + 36$
    D. $x^2 - 36$

24. Find $(x-3)(x+3)$.
    A. $x^2 + 9$
    B. $x^2 - 6x - 9$
    C. $x^2 - 9$
    D. $x^2 - 6x + 9$

25. Suppose the perimeter of a triangle is given by $P = 13x + 6y$, and two of its sides have lengths of $3x + 2y$ and $7x + 3y$. What is the length of the third side?
    A. $6x + 3y$
    B. $23x + 5y$
    C. $3x$
    D. $3x + y$

26. Find the product $(2x + 3)(3x - 2)$.
    A. $6x^2 + 5x - 5$
    B. $6x^2 + 5x - 6$
    C. $6x^2 + 9x - 6$
    D. $6x^2 + 9x - 5$

POLYNOMIAL FUNCTIONS

27. Find number of terms for $(4x^2 + 3x) + (7x^2 - 5x - 6)$.
    A. 2
    B. 5
    C. 3
    D. 6

28. Find the difference $(-3x^3 - 7x^2 + 5x - 4) - (6x^2 - 8)$.
    A. $-11x^8 + 4$
    B. $-3x^3 - 13x^2 + 5x + 4$
    C. $-3x^3 - x^2 + 5x - 12$
    D. $-3x^3 - 13x^2 + 5x - 12$

29. Find $(2y^2 + 7y - 5)(3y^2 - 5y + 4)$.
    A. $5y^2 + 2y - 1$
    B. $6y^4 - 35y^2 - 20$
    C. $6y^4 + 4y^2 - 32y^2 - 20$
    D. $6y^4 + 11y^3 - 42y^2 + 53y - 20$

30. Suppose that the base of a triangle is $3xy$ and its height is also $3xy$. What is its area, expressed as a monomial?
    A. $\frac{9}{2}x^4$
    B. $6x^2y^2$
    C. x^4
    D. $\frac{9}{2}x^2 y^2$

POLYNOMIAL FUNCTIONS

31. Write a polynomial to represent the area of a rectangle which has length 5 more than width, assume length 'x'.
    A. $x^2 - 5x$
    B. $4x$
    C. $x^2 - 2x + 5$
    D. $x^2 - 10x$

32. Which of the following expressions is written in standard form?
    A. $3x^4 + 5x^3 - 7x - 3$
    B. $x + 2x^3 - 2x^2 - 5x^4$
    C. $x + 2x^3 + 5x^4$
    D. $x + 1 - 6x^3 + 2x^4$

33. Multiply $4x^2(-x^2 - 3x + 2)$.
    A. $-4x^4 - 12x^3 + 8x^2$
    B. $-4x^4 - 7x^3 + 8x^2$
    C. $-4x^2 - 12x + 8$
    D. $-4x^2 - 7x + 8$

34. A rectangle has a base of $4x - 1$ and a height of $3x + 2$. What is the area?
    A. $12x^2 - 5x - 2$
    B. $12x^2 + 5x - 2$
    C. $12x^2 - 5x + 2$
    D. $12x^2 + 5x + 2$

POLYNOMIAL FUNCTIONS

35. The length of one side of a square is $x + 4$. What is the area?
    A. $x^2 + 8x + 8$
    B. $x^2 + 8x + 16$
    C. $2x + 8$
    D. $x^2 + 4x + 16$

36. Find the product $(4n + 3)(4n - 3)$.
    A. $16n^2 - 9$
    B. $16n^2 - 24n - 9$
    C. $16n^2 + 24n - 9$
    D. $16n^2 + 9$

37. Simplify:
    $(3x^2 - 2x + 1) - (x^2 - 2x - 3) + (4x^2 - x + 2)$
    A. $6x^2 - x + 6$
    B. $6x^2 - 5x + 6$
    C. $6x^2 - x$
    D. $8x^2 - 5x + 6$

38. Find the value of b.

    $$9x^2 + bx - 21 = 3(3x^2 + 2x - 7)$$

    Record your answer in the space provided below.

POLYNOMIAL FUNCTIONS

39. Factor: $2(3-m) - 3m(m-3)$
    A. $(2-3m)(m-3)$
    B. $(2+3m)(m-3)$
    C. $(2+3m)(3-m)$
    D. $(6-2m)(m-3)$

40. Selena is using her Mac book to design invitations to her graduation party. The text of the invitation is contained in a rectangle with a length of 11.5 inches and a width of 7 inches. Around the perimeter of the text, Selena wants to have a blue border of width b. Around the blue border, she wants a pink border of width p. Find an expression for the perimeter of the completed invitation.

a. 18.5	b. 36	c. 37	d. 2
e. 4	f. 6	g. 8	h. 0

    From the options above, record one correct answer in each box. Not all answers need to be used.

    Perimeter P = ☐ + ☐ b + ☐ p

41. Factor $5(x-2) - 9x(x-2)$.
    A. $-45x(x-2)$
    B. $(x-2)(9x-5)$
    C. $(5-9x)(x-2)(x-2)$
    D. $(x-2)(5-9x)$

POLYNOMIAL FUNCTIONS

42. Divide. Simplify your answer.
$(12x^4 - 18x^3 + 36x^2) \div (6x^3)$

A. $12x - 18 + \frac{36}{x}$

B. $2x - 3 + \frac{6}{x}$

C. $2x^4 - 3x^3 + 6x^2$

D. $6x - \frac{12}{x^2} + \frac{30}{x^3}$

43. Divide $(8y^4 - 8y^2 + 2)$ by $4y^3$.

A. $\frac{2}{y} + \frac{1}{2y^3}$

B. $\frac{2}{y} - 2y + 2y^3$

C. $2y - \frac{2}{y} + \frac{1}{2y^3}$

D. $2y - 8y^2 + 2$

44. A company distributes its product by flight and by truck. The cost of distributing by flight can be modeled as $-0.09x^2 + 34x - 100$, and the cost of distributing by trucks can be modeled as $-0.04x^2 + 22x - 175$, where x is the number of tons of product distributed. Write a polynomial that represents the difference between the cost of distributing by flight and the cost of distributing by trucks.

A. $-0.05x^2 + 56x - 275$

B. $-0.13x^2 + 12x - 275$

C. $-0.05x^2 + 12x + 75$

D. $-0.05x^2 + 12x - 27$

POLYNOMIAL FUNCTIONS

45. Divide $(15a^4 + 20a^3 - 5a^2)$ by $-5a$.
    A. $10a^3 + 15a^2 - a$
    B. $-3a^3 - 4a^2 + a$
    C. $3a^4 - 4a^2 + 5a$
    D. $-10a^3 - 15a^2 - a$

46. Factor.
    $24u^5 + 66u^4 + 45u^3$
    A. $3u^3(2u + 5)(4u + 3)$
    B. $u^3(2u - 5)(4u + 3)$
    C. $u^3(4u + 5)(2u + 3)$
    D. $3u^3(4u + 5)(2u + 3)$

47. Subtract $(6a^2 + 3a) - 0.5(4a^2 + 2a)$.
    A. $4a^2 + 2a$
    B. $2a^2 - 2a$
    C. $4a^2 - 2a$
    D. $3a^3$

48. Multiply: $(3a + 2b)(3a - 2b)$
    A. $9a^2 + 6ab - 4b^2$
    B. $9a^2 + 4b^2$
    C. $9a^2 - 4b^2$
    D. $9a^2 - 6ab - 4b^2$

POLYNOMIAL FUNCTIONS

49. Divide: $(18x^3 + 9x^2) \div (3x)$

    A. $6x^2 + 3$
    B. $6x^2 + 3x$
    C. $3x^2 + 3x$
    D. $6x^3 + 3x$

50. Roddick divides a trinomial by a monomial, as shown below. What will be the quotient?

    $$\frac{3x^4 + 9x^2 + 15x}{3x}$$

    A. $x^3 + 9x^2 + 15x$
    B. $x^4 + 3x^2 + 5x$
    C. $x^3 + 3x + 5$
    D. $3x^4 + 9x^2 + 5$

51. Simplify $\frac{14c^3d^2 - 21c^2d^3}{14cd}$

    A. $c^2 - \frac{3cd}{2}$
    B. $c^2 - \frac{3c^2d}{2}$
    C. $c^2 - 21c^2d^3$
    D. $c^2d - \frac{3cd^2}{2}$

POLYNOMIAL FUNCTIONS

52. Which expression is equivalent to the following expression?

$\frac{1}{2}x(4x - 6) + 3(x^2 - 1)$

A. $5x^2 - 3x + 3$
B. $x^2 + 3x - 6$
C. $5x^2 - 3x - 3$
D. $-x^2 + 3x + 3$

53. Sebastian wants to simplify the following:

$$\frac{20x^2 + 5x}{5x}$$

Record your answer in the space below.

54. The area of a parallelogram is $35p^6q^6$ square units. If the base of the parallelogram measures $5pq^2$ units, what is the height of the parallelogram? ($p > 0$ and $q > 0$)

A. $7p^5q^4$ units
B. $7p^6q^3$ units
C. $30p^5q^4$ units
D. $30p^6q^3$ units

POLYNOMIAL FUNCTIONS

55. The side length of a square is $4x^3yz^4$ units. What is the area of the square?
    - A. $8x^6y^2z^8$ square units
    - B. $8x^9yz^{16}$ square units
    - C. $16x^6y^2z^8$ square units
    - D. $16x^9yz^{16}$ square units

56. Select one correct answer from each box for the given polynomial.
$$\frac{(2x^2)(8x^6)}{4x^6}$$

    Given Polynomial is [A. Monomial / B. Binomial / C. Trinomial] and has coefficient as [D. 2 / E. 4 / F. 8]

57. What is the degree of following polynomial?
$$\frac{20x^2 + 5x}{5x}$$

58. Find leading coefficient of $(12x^4 - 18x^3 + 36x^2) \div (6x^3)$

POLYNOMIAL FUNCTIONS

59. Which one is not a polynomial?

    A. $\dfrac{3+5x}{\sqrt{3}}$

    B. $\dfrac{5}{x-2}$

    C. $-x^2 + 3x + 3$

    D. $-2y^2 + 0.8y$

60. If $g = x^2$, $h = x - 1$ then which one is not polynomial:

    A. $g + h$

    B. $g - h$

    C. $g \times h$

    D. $\dfrac{g}{h}$

61. Find GCF of following polynomial.

    $36a^2b^2c^4, 54a^5c^2, 90a^4b^2c^2$

    A. 6abc

    B. $9a^2b^2c^4$

    C. $18a^2b^2$

    D. $18a^2c^2$

62. Find GCF of following polynomial.

    $12m^2n^2$, 6mn and $3n^2$

    A. $3mn^2$

    B. 12m

    C. 3m

    D. 3n

POLYNOMIAL FUNCTIONS

63. Find the area of the figure below.

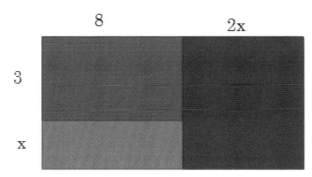

A. $24 + 2x^2$
B. $2x^2 + 14x + 24$
C. $8x + 2x^2$
D. $3x + 11$

64. A rectangular prism has the volume V (x) = $2x^3 + 9x^2 + 4x - 15$. Find the depth of the prism if the length of the prism is (2x+ 5) and width is (x + 3).

A. x – 1
B. 2x + 3
C. x + 1
D. not enough information

POLYNOMIAL FUNCTIONS

65. A company used the function r(x) = 5x +15,000 to predict the amount of revenue they will earn next year. Company uses the function c(x) = 2x − 2000 to predict the amount they will spend in costs next year. Which function shows the amount of profit p(x) the company predicts to earn after cost? Select one correct answer from each box below.

   Profit is calculated by using

   A. r(x) + c(x)
   B. c(x) − r(x)
   C. r(x) − c(x)

   and profit is

   A. 7x + 13000
   B. 3x + 13000
   C. 7x + 17000
   D. 3x + 17000

66. The polynomial $x^2 - 7x + 15$ models the profit a company makes on selling an item at a price x. A second item sold at the same price brings in a profit of $3x^2 + 4x - 50$. Which of the following polynomial expresses the total profit from the sale of both items?

   A. 4x² + 3x − 35
   B. 2x² + 11x − 65
   C. 4x² - 3x − 35
   D. 2x² + 3x − 65

67. Serena has a triangular shaped garden with a perimeter that can be represented by $25r^2 - 9r + 14$. The sum of two sides of the garden is represented by $10r^2 + 12r + 9$. Which expression represents the length of the third side?

   A. 15r² +3r + 23
   B. 15r² - 21r + 5
   C. 15r² -3r - 5
   D. 15r² - 21r + 23

POLYNOMIAL FUNCTIONS

68. A box is created from a sheet of cardboard 20 in. on a side by cutting a square from each corner and folding up the sides. Let x represent the length of the sides of the squares removed from each corner. Find an expression for the volume of the box in terms of x.

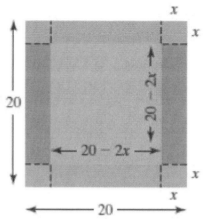

  A. $(20 - 2x)(20 - 2x)$
  B. $x(20 - 2x)(20 - 2x)$
  C. $2x(20 - 2x)(20 - 2x)$
  D. $x(40 - 4x)$

69. Which one is not a polynomial?
  A. $4x^2 + 2x - 1$
  B. $y + \dfrac{3}{y}$
  C. $x^3 - 1$
  D. $y^2 + 5y + 1$

POLYNOMIAL FUNCTIONS

70. The cost of a video game can be modeled by the equation C = 5x + 22. The number of games sold can be modeled by the equation N = 9x − 7. Write a model for the revenue from the sale of the games.

    A. (5x + 22)+(9x − 7)
    B. (5x + 22) - (9x − 7)
    C. (5x + 22)(9x − 7)
    D. (5x + 22)÷(9x − 7)

Answer Key – Polynomial Functions

		Marks (C/W)			Marks (C/W)			Marks (C/W)
1	B		31	A		61	D	
2	B		32	A		62	D	
3	A		33	A		63	B	
4	D		34	B		64	A	
5	B		35	B		65	C, D	
6	B		36	A		66	C	
7	A		37	A		67	B	
8	D		38	6		68	B	
9	A		39	C		69	B	
10	A		40	C, G, G		70	C	
11	D		41	D				
12	D		42	B				
13	C		43	C				
14	B		44	C				
15	D		45	B				
16	C		46	D				
17	C		47	A				
18	D		48	C				
19	B		49	B				
20	B		50	C				
21	A		51	D				
22	B		52	C				
23	B		53	4x+1				
24	C		54	A				
25	D		55	C				
26	B		56	A, E				
27	C		57	1				
28	B		58	2				
29	D		59	B				
30	D		60	D				
Total			Total			Total		

SECTION 7

QUADRATIC FUNCTIONS

QUADRATIC FUNCTIONS

1. The equation $x^2 - 6 = -2x$ does not have integer roots. State the consecutive integers between which the roots lie.
    A. between 0 and 1 and between 2 and 3
    B. between -4 and -3 and between 1 and 2
    C. between -3 and -2 and between 0 and 1
    D. between -1 and 0 and between 0 and 1

2. Solve for x, $x^2 + 2x - 8 = 0$.
    A. -2
    B. -4, 2
    C. -4, -2
    D. -4

3. Find zeros for $y = 2x^2 + 7x + 4$. Approximate the solutions to the nearest hundredth.
    A. -2.78, -0.72
    B. -3.35, -0.15
    C. 1.28, 3.66
    D. -5.24, -1.90

4. Find x-intercept of $y = x^2 - 16x - 17$
    A. {1, 13}
    B. {1, 17}
    C. {−1, 17}
    D. {−1, 13}

QUADRATIC FUNCTIONS

5. What is the equation of the graph shown?

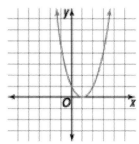

   A. $y = x^2 - 2x + 1$
   B. $y = -x^2 + 2x - 1$
   C. $y = -x^2 - 2x - 1$
   D. $y = x^2 + 2x + 1$

6. Find the value of b that makes $x^2 + bx + 36$ a perfect square.
   A. 12
   B. -12, 12
   C. 6
   D. 324

7. Solve for x, $x^2 - 12x + 34 = 0$.
   A. $\sqrt{2} \pm 6$
   B. $6 \pm \sqrt{2}$
   C. {5, 7}
   D. {6}

QUADRATIC FUNCTIONS

8. Which method of solving quadratic equations is best suited for the equation $x^2 - 18x = 0$

   A. factoring
   B. completing the square
   C. graphing
   D. quadratic formula

9. What is the equation of the graph shown?

   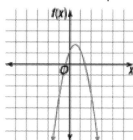

   A. $f(x) = 2x^2 + 2x + 1$
   B. $f(x) = -2x^2 + 2x - 1$
   C. $f(x) = 2x^2 - 2x + 1$
   D. $f(x) = -2x^2 + 2x + 1$

QUADRATIC FUNCTIONS

10. What are the real roots of the quadratic equation whose related function is graphed below?

    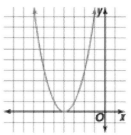

    A. -4, 4
    B. -4
    C. -2
    D. 4

11. Find zeros of $y = x^2 - 4x + 1$.

    A. $2 \pm \sqrt{5}$
    B. $2 \pm \sqrt{3}$
    C. -1, -3
    D. 1, 3

12. Which of the following equations will have exactly 1 real root?

    A. $4x^2 - 8x + 4$
    B. $x^2 - 6x - 9$
    C. $2x^2 + 5x - 16$
    D. $9x^2 + 12x - 4$

QUADRATIC FUNCTIONS

13. Solve $5x^2 - 10x = 0$.
    A. $x = 0$ or $x = -2$
    B. $x = 0$ or $x = 2$
    C. $x = 2$
    D. $x = 0$

14. Factor $6y^2 + 22y - 8$.
    A. $2(3y - 1)(y + 4)$
    B. $(6y - 1)(y + 8)$
    C. $2(3y - 2)(y + 2)$
    D. $(2y - 4)(3y + 2)$

15. Which expression shows one of the factors of $4y^2 - 9$?
    A. $4y - 9$
    B. $(2y + 3)$
    C. $2y^2 - 3$
    D. All of the above

16. Which of the following trinomials is a perfect square trinomial?
    A. $9a^2 - 12a + 4$
    B. $4y^2 + 10y + 25$
    C. $x^2 + 16x + 16$
    D. $r^2 - 6r + 36$

QUADRATIC FUNCTIONS

17. Which equation shows vertex form for following graph?

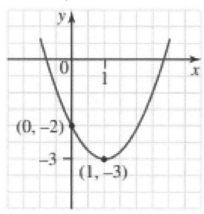

A. $y = 3(x + 1)^2 - 3$
B. $y = (x + 1)^2 - 3$
C. $y = (x - 1)^2 - 3$
D. $y = 2(x - 1)^2 - 3$

18. Solve $4y^2 - 25 = 0$.

A. $y = -\frac{5}{2}$
B. $y = \frac{25}{4}$
C. $y = \frac{5}{2}$
D. $y = -\frac{5}{2} \, or \, y = \frac{5}{2}$

QUADRATIC FUNCTIONS

19. Which equation shows vertex form for following graph?

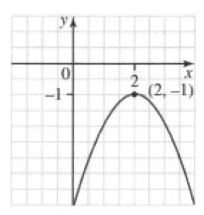

A. y = (x - 2)² – 1
B. y = -2(x + 2)² – 1
C. y = -(x - 2)² – 1
D. y = -2(x - 2)² – 1

20. Solve for x.

    $x^2 - 9x = 0$

    A. $-9, 9$
    B. $0, 9$
    C. $0, -9$
    D. 9

QUADRATIC FUNCTIONS

21. Solve for x.

    $40x^2 - 76x + 28 = 0$

    A. $-\dfrac{1}{2}, \dfrac{7}{5}$

    B. $\dfrac{1}{2}, \dfrac{7}{5}$

    C. $\dfrac{4}{5}, \dfrac{7}{8}$

    D. $-\dfrac{4}{5}, \dfrac{7}{8}$

22. Look at the equations shown below.

    $$y = \dfrac{4}{5}x^2 + 13, \quad y = -\dfrac{2}{5}x^2, \quad y = \dfrac{1}{5}x^2 - 5, \quad y = \dfrac{1}{8}x^2 + \dfrac{3}{5}$$

    Which of the following statements are true for the graphs of all the equations given? Select all applicable answers.

    A. The graphs are congruent and open downward.

    B. The graphs open upwards.

    C. The graphs are listed from narrowest to widest.

    D. The graphs open upward and are symmetrical about the x-axis.

    E. The graphs are symmetrical about the y-axis.

QUADRATIC FUNCTIONS

23. Use the graph to find x-intercept and y-intercept of $x^2 - 2x - 3 = 0$.

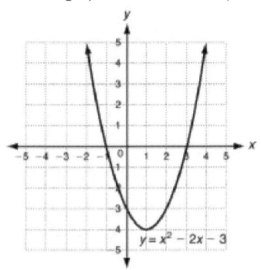

A. (0,3), (0,-1), (0,-3)
B. (-1,0), (3,0), (0,-3)
C. (-1,0), (3,0), (0,-4)
D. (1,0), (3,0), (0,-3)

24. Factor $5(x-2) - 9x(x-2)$.
A. $-45x(x-2)$
B. $(x-2)(9x-5)$
C. $(5-9x)(x-2)(x-2)$
D. $(x-2)(5-9x)$

25. Factor $x^2 - 16$.
A. $(x-4)^2$
B. $(x+4)(x-4)$
C. $(x+4)^2$
D. cannot be factored

QUADRATIC FUNCTIONS

26. Find the value of a.

    $4x^2 + ax = 2x(2x + 1)$

    Record your answer in the space provided below.

27. If you graph $y = x^2 - 6x + 9$, the y-intercept of the graph of the equation is _____.

    A. −3
    B. 9
    C. 2
    D. 0

QUADRATIC FUNCTIONS

28. The height of a ball in feet is modeled by $y = -16x^2 + 72x$, where x is the time in seconds after the ball is hit. How long is the ball in the air?

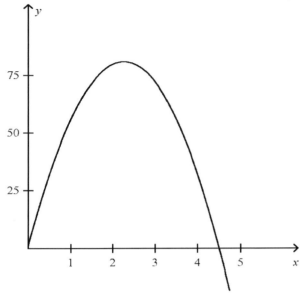

A. 2.25 s

B. 4.5 s

C. 9 s

D. 81 s

29. Find Y coordinate the vertex of $y = -2x^2 + 4x - 3$ and tell whether it is a maximum or minimum.

Select one correct statement from each box below to complete the sentence.

The given function has a
- Maximum
- Minimum

and Y coordinate of vertex is

A. 3
B. 9
C. -1
D. -3

QUADRATIC FUNCTIONS

30. Find axis of symmetry for $y = x^2 + 4x + 4$.

    A. $x = -2$

    B. $x = 4$

    C. $x = 2$

    D. $x = -4$

31. What are the roots for the quadratic equation $x^2 + 6x = 16$?

    A. $\{-2, -8\}$

    B. $\{-2, 8\}$

    C. $\{2, -8\}$

    D. $\{2, 8\}$

32. What is the solution set of the quadratic equation $8x^2 + 2x + 1 = y$?

    A. $\left\{-\frac{1}{2}, \frac{1}{4}\right\}$

    B. $\{-1 + \sqrt{2}, -1 - \sqrt{2}\}$

    C. $\left\{\frac{-1+\sqrt{7}}{8}, \frac{-1-\sqrt{7}}{8}\right\}$

    D. no real solution

QUADRATIC FUNCTIONS

33. The function below can be used to describe the path of a bird flying.
$$f(x) = -x^2 - 4x + 32$$

What is the maximum height bird could achieve where x represent time in sec and f(x) shows height of the bird in yd.

A. 20 yd

B. 32 yd

C. 36 yd

D. Can't determine

QUADRATIC FUNCTIONS

34. Which of the following is the graph of the function $y = x^2 + 2x - 3$?

A.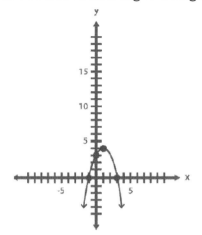

C.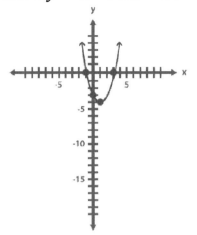

B.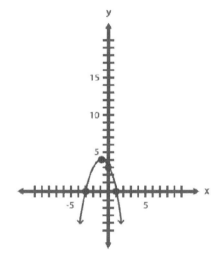

D.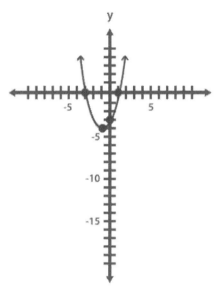

QUADRATIC FUNCTIONS

35. Niang needs to solve the problem below using the quadratic formula.
$$x^2 + 8x + 7 = -8$$
Which use of the following shows the quadratic formula being used correctly to determine the solutions for this problem?

   A. $x = \dfrac{-8 \pm \sqrt{8^2 - 4(1)(7)}}{2(1)}$

   B. $x = \dfrac{-8 \pm \sqrt{8^2 - 4(1)(-8)}}{2(1)}$

   C. $x = \dfrac{8 \pm \sqrt{8^2 - 4(1)(15)}}{2(1)}$

   D. $x = \dfrac{-8 \pm \sqrt{8^2 - 4(1)(15)}}{2(1)}$

36. Solve the following: $(q + 2)^2 = 25$.

   A. {3}

   B. {–3, 3}

   C. {–7, 3}

   D. {–7}

37. Which expression is factor of $5x^2 + 13x - 6$?

   A. not factorable

   B. $(x - 2)$

   C. $(x + 3)$

   D. $(5x + 2)$

QUADRATIC FUNCTIONS

38. Determine whether the trinomial $9x^2 - 60x + 25$ is a perfect square trinomial. If so, determine the factor.
    A. Yes, $(3x + 5)(3x - 5)$
    B. It is prime
    C. Yes, $(3x + 15)(3x - 15)$
    D. Yes, $(9x + 15)(x - 15)$

39. Which is factor form of the equation $x^2 - \frac{6x}{5} + \frac{9}{25} = 0$.
    A. $(x - \frac{3}{5})(x - \frac{3}{5}) = 0$
    B. $(x + \frac{3}{5})(x + \frac{3}{5}) = 0$
    C. $(x - \frac{3}{5})(x + \frac{3}{5}) = 0$
    D. $(3x - \frac{3}{5})(3x - \frac{3}{5}) = 0$

40. Factor $3x^3 + 2x^2y + 3xy^2 + 2y^3$
    A. $(x^2 + y^2)(3x + 2y)$
    B. $x^2(3x + 2y) + y^2(3x + 2y)$
    C. $xy(3x^2 + 2x + 3y + 2y^2)$
    D. $(3x + 2y)(x + y)(x - y)$

41. Factor $2x^5 - 98x^3$
    A. $2x^3(x + 7)(x - 7)$
    B. $2x^2(x - 7)(x - 7)$
    C. $2x^4(x + 7)(x + 7)$
    D. $2x^3(x + 49)(x - 49)$

QUADRATIC FUNCTIONS

42. Solve $a^2 - 12a = -27$.

    A. $a = 9$

    B. $a = 3$

    C. $a = 3$ or $a = 9$

    D. $a = -27$ or $a = -15$

43. Factor $4x^2 - 14x - 8$.

    A. $(2x + 1)(x - 4)$

    B. $2(2x + 1)(x - 2)$

    C. $2(2x + 1)(x - 4)$

    D. $(2x + 1)(x - 2)$

44. Write the factored form of $x^2 - \frac{2}{3}x + \frac{1}{9} = 0$. Also write number of zeros.

    Select one correct answer from each boxed below.

    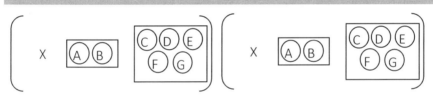

    Number of zeros

45. An expression for the area of a rectangle is $xy - 2x + 3y - 6$. Express this area in factored form.

    Record your answer in the space provided below.

QUADRATIC FUNCTIONS

46. Factor $6y^2 + 22y - 8$.
    A. $2(3y - 2)(y + 2)$
    B. $(6y - 1)(y + 8)$
    C. $2(3y - 1)(y + 4)$
    D. $(2y - 4)(3y + 2)$

47. Factor $4y^2 - 9$.
    A. prime
    B. $(2y + 3)(2y - 3)$
    C. $(2y - 3)(2y - 3)$
    D. $(2y + 3)(2y + 3)$

48. Which of the following trinomials is NOT a perfect square trinomial?
    A. $9a^2 - 6a + 1$
    B. $4y^2 + 10y + 25$
    C. $x^2 + 8x + 16$
    D. $r^2 - 12r + 36$

49. Solve $3x^2 + 5 = 8x$.
    A. $x = \frac{5}{3}$ or $x = 1$
    B. $x = 5$ or $x = 1$
    C. $x = 0$
    D. $x = 1$

QUADRATIC FUNCTIONS

50. Factor $81x^2 - 225$.
    A. $9(9x - 25)(9x + 25)$
    B. $9(9x - 5)(9x + 5)$
    C. $9(3x - 5)(3x + 5)$
    D. $3(3x - 5)(3x + 5)$

51. How many real solutions does $f(x) = 0.25x^2 + 8 - x\sqrt{8}$ have?
    A. 0
    B. 1
    C. 2
    D. Not enough information

52. Factor $3x^3 + 3x^2 - 12x - 12$.
    A. $3(x - 2)(x + 2)(x + 1)$
    B. $(x - 2)(x + 2)(x + 1)$
    C. $(x - 2)(x - 2)(x + 1)$
    D. $3(x - 2)(x - 2)(x + 1)$

53. How many solutions does $f(x) = 4y^2 - 25$ have?
    A. 0
    B. 1
    C. 2
    D. Not enough information

QUADRATIC FUNCTIONS

54. A cannonball is fired with an initial velocity of 100 meters per second. The object's distance, d, above the ground at any time, t, can be represented by the equation $d = 100t - 5t^2$. When will the cannonball be 600 meters above the ground?

    A. $t = 10$ sec
    B. $t = 5$ sec, $t = 15$ sec
    C. $t = 8.6$ sec, $t = 11.4$ sec
    D. The cannonball will never reach 600 meters.

55. Arrange following quadratic function from wider to narrower.

    $$\frac{2}{5}x^2, \frac{1}{2}x^2, -2x^2, -7x^2, \frac{-4}{9}x^2$$

    A. $\frac{2}{5}x^2, -\frac{4}{9}x^2, \frac{1}{2}x^2, -2x^2, -7x^2$
    B. $-2x^2, -7x^2, \frac{2}{5}x^2, -\frac{4}{9}x^2, \frac{1}{2}x^2$
    C. $-7x^2, -2x^2, -\frac{4}{9}x^2, \frac{2}{5}x^2, \frac{1}{2}x^2$
    D. None of the above

56. Write an equation of a graph g(x) that is narrower and translated 7 units down than the graph of $f(x) = \frac{1}{2}x^2 + 5$.

    A. $g(x) = \frac{1}{2}x^2 + 12$
    B. $g(x) = \frac{5}{4}x^2 - 2$
    C. $g(x) = 2x^2 + 2$
    D. $g(x) = \frac{1}{4}x^2 - 2$

QUADRATIC FUNCTIONS

57. Write an equation of a graph that is reflected and translated 2 units right than the graph of $f(x) = 4x^2$.

   Record your answer in the space provided below.

   ☐

58. How does the quadratic function $y = -(x+2)^2$ compare to its parent function?
   A. It is less steep, reflected and moves 2 units to the left.
   B. It is reflected and moves 2 units to the right.
   C. It is reflected and moves 2 units to the left.
   D. It moves 2 unit to the left.

59. The axis of symmetry for the graph shown below is

   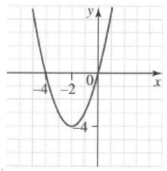

   A. x=2
   B. x=-2
   C. x=-4
   D. y=0

QUADRATIC FUNCTIONS

60. For what value of K does that equation $2x^2 - kx + 8 = 0$ have one real root?

    A. 0
    B. 4
    C. 4, -4
    D. 8, -8

61. What number must you add to $x^2 + 18x$ to create a perfect Square?

    A. 18
    B. 9
    C. 81
    D. 8

62. If a quadratic function is expressed in vertex form
    $f(x) = a(x - h)^2 + k$, then which of the following statements are true?

    A. Equation of axis of symmetry is x = h
    B. Function has maximum value of k when a < 0
    C. Function has minimum value of k when a < 0
    D. Y-intercept of given equation is (0, k)
    E. Vertex coordinate is (h, k)

63. Compared to the graph of $f(x) = x^2$, the graph of $g(x) = 2x^2 - 5$ is _____.

    A. narrower and translated down
    B. narrower and translated up
    C. wider and translated down
    D. wider and translated up

QUADRATIC FUNCTIONS

64. Which transformation from the graph of a function $f(x)$ describes the graph of $\frac{1}{3}f(x)$?

    A. horizontal shift left $\frac{1}{3}$ unit

    B. vertical shift up $\frac{1}{3}$ unit

    C. vertical compression by a factor of $\frac{1}{3}$

    D. vertical shift down $\frac{1}{3}$ unit

65. Which is the graph of $y = -2(x-2)^2 - 4$?

    A.
    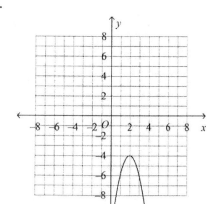

    B.
    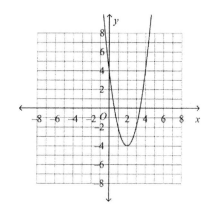

    C.
    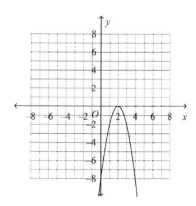

    D.
    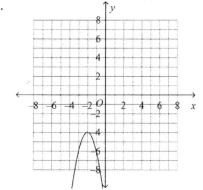

QUADRATIC FUNCTIONS

66. Find the number and type of solutions for $x^2 - 9x = -8$.

    A. Cannot determine without graphing.

    B. The equation has one real solution.

    C. The equation has two non-real complex solutions.

    D. The equation has two real solutions.

67. Find the vertex and y-intercept of $y = 5x^2 + 9x - 2$.

    A. vertex: (-9, 5), y-intercept: (0,-2)

    B. vertex: $\left(-\frac{9}{10}, \frac{-121}{20}\right)$, y-intercept: (0,-2)

    C. vertex: $\left(-\frac{9}{2}, -\frac{109}{25}\right)$, y-intercept: (-2,0)

    D. vertex: $\left(\frac{9}{10}, \frac{137}{50}\right)$, y-intercept: (-2,0)

68. The height of an arrow that is shot upward at an initial velocity of 40 meters per second can be modeled by $h = 40t - 5t^2$, where h is the height in meters and t is the time in seconds. Find the time it takes for the arrow to reach the ground.

69. You toss a ball that travels on the path $y = -0.1x^2 + x + 2$ where x and y are measured in meters. At what time ball will reach to its maximum height?

QUADRATIC FUNCTIONS

70. The table of values below is for a parabola.

x	-7	-6	-5	-4	-3	-2	-1	0	1	2
y	-4	-9	-12	-13	-12	-9	-4	3	12	23

What is y-coordinates of the vertex?

71. What is standard form of equation $f(x) = 3(x-4)^2 - 6$?
    A. $f(x) = 3x^2 - 24x + 42$
    B. $f(x) = 4x^2 - 18x + 48$
    C. $f(x) = 3x^2 - 24x + 48$
    D. $f(x) = 4x^2 - 21x + 36$

72. The axis of symmetry of a parabola is at x = -2. If one x-intercept is (6, 0), what is the other x-intercept?
    A. (10,0)
    B. (-10,0)
    C. (-6,0)
    D. (-2,0)

73. The product of two consecutive positive even integers is 14 more than their sum. Which equation can be used to find the integers?
    A. x(x + 1) = 14 + x + 2
    B. x(x + 1) = 14 + 2x + 2
    C. x(x + 2) = 14 + x
    D. x(x + 2) = 14 + 2x + 2

QUADRATIC FUNCTIONS

74. Garry's school holds a fundraiser to benefit organizations treating diabetes patients. For each student that participates in the fundraiser, the school donates $10. In addition, the students obtain a pledge of $7 from each donor they find. The graph of Garry's contribution in terms of the number of donors she finds is shown below.

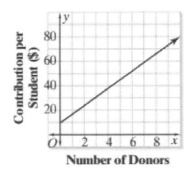

If the contribution of each donor were increased to $9, how would the graph change?

A. The slope would increase, causing the line to rise more steeply.
B. The line would cross the y-axis at (0, 9) rather than (0, 10).
C. The line would cross the x-axis at (9, 0).
D. The slope would decrease, causing the line to rise less steeply.

QUADRATIC FUNCTIONS

75. A phone company charges $30.00 per month plus $0.10 for every minute of long-distance phone calls. The total charge is graphed below.

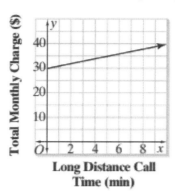

Which of the following would increase the charge per long distance minute to $0.20?

A. Halving the y-intercept
B. Doubling the y-intercept
C. Halving the slope
D. Doubling the slope

QUADRATIC FUNCTIONS

Answer Key – Quadratic Functions

		Marks (C/W)
1	B	
2	B	
3	A	
4	C	
5	A	
6	B	
7	B	
8	A	
9	D	
10	B	
11	B	
12	A	
13	B	
14	A	
15	B	
16	A	
17	C	
18	D	
19	C	
20	B	
21	B	
22	C, E	
23	B	
24	D	
25	B	
26	2	
27	B	
28	B	
29	Maximum, C	
30	A	
	Total	

		Marks (C/W)
31	C	
32	D	
33	C	
34	D	
35	D	
36	C	
37	C	
38	B	
39	A	
40	A	
41	A	
42	C	
43	C	
44	BC, BC, 1	
45	$(x+3)(y-2)$	
46	C	
47	B	
48	B	
49	A	
50	C	
51	B	
52	A	
53	C	
54	D	
55	A	
56	B	
57	$g(x) = -4(x-2)^2$	
58	C	
59	B	
60	D	
	Total	

		Marks (C/W)
61	C	
62	A, B, E	
63	A	
64	C	
65	A	
66	D	
67	B	
68	8	
69	5	
70	-13	
71	A	
72	B	
73	D	
74	A	
75	D	
76		
77		
78		
79		
80		
81		
82		
83		
84		
85		
86		
87		
88		
89		
90		
	Total	

SOLUTIONS

Section 1- Linear equations and inequality

- **Section 1 - Question 2** - To write the mathematical equivalent of the sentence given, we have to start from the left, the sum of -29 and 28. This is written as -29 + 28. Then the next part says, this is -7 more than a number, which can be written as -7 + x, x being that unknown number. Equating, we get

  $$-29 + 28 = -7 + x \quad \text{combine like terms}$$
  $$-1 = -7 + x \quad \text{Add + 7 to both sides}$$
  $$6 = x$$

- **Section 1 – Question 4** - Total earning for Frost includes the $15 and another 10 cents for each flyer. If he distributes x flyers, he gets paid $0.10x, so the total payment he gets is 15 + 0.10x $. He wants to make at least $85 each day in other words he wants to earn a minimum of $85 or more. So, 15 + 0.10x ≥ 85

  $$\boxed{C}$$

- **Section 1 – Question 5** - Total salary from MNC company = 48000.
  PQR Company is offering 2% commission on sales, s. This can be written as 0.02s, so the total earnings from PQR is 41,000 + .02s. Based on question we can write:

  $$41,000 + 0.02s > 48,000$$
  $$0.02s > 7,000$$
  $$s > 350,000 \quad \boxed{D}$$

- **Section 1 – Question 10** - First we have to apply distributive property.

$3(5 + 2n) \geq 7 + 10n$	distributive property
$15 + 6n \geq 7 + 10n$	Subtract 6n from both sides
$15 \geq 7+4n$	Subtract 7 from both sides
$8 \geq 4n$	Divide by 2 on both sides
$2 \geq n$ OR $n \leq 2$	$\boxed{C}$

- **Section 1 – Question 13** - We have to solve two sets of inequalities

$8x - 21 < 2x$	$3x + 5 \geq -1$
$6x - 21 < 0$	$3x \geq -6$
$6x < 21$	$x \geq -2$
$x < 3.5$	

  Combining the two we get, $-2 \leq x < 3.5$

  $$\boxed{B, E}$$

SOLUTIONS

❖ Section 1 – Question 33 –

$\frac{1}{2} - \frac{2}{3}x < \frac{5}{6}$ Let us make all the fractions with the same denominator.

$\frac{3}{6} - \frac{4}{6}x < \frac{5}{6}$ Multiply each term by 6 on both sides

3 – 4x < 5   Subtract 3 from both sides

-4x < 2   Divide by negative 4

x > -0.5   Flip the inequality, whenever we multiply/divide by a negative number

$\boxed{A}$

❖ Section 1 – Question 37 - If the cost of 1 tulip is $5, then the cost of x tulips is 5x.

If the cost of 1 carnation is $3, then the cost of y carnations is 3y.

The total of these two should not go above $45 which implies it can be less than or equal to 45.

$$5x + 3y \leq 45$$

$\boxed{F, E, D, H}$

❖ Section 1 – Question 45 –

|-x -2y| Substitute x = -12 and y = 8

| -(-12) – 2 (8) |

= |12 – 16 |

= |-4| =   4

$\boxed{A}$

❖ Section 1 – Question 49 - To write an equation in the form y = mx + b we should know the slope m and y intercept 'b'. Look at the table, the y intercept is the value of y, when x = 0. In this problem y intercept 'b' = -4. Slope can be calculated using the formula m = $\frac{y_2 - y_1}{y_2 - x_1}$

Take any two sets of co-ordinate pairs. (3, 2) and (2, 0)

$\frac{2 - 0}{3 - 2} = \frac{2}{1} = 2$

So, the equation is y = 2x – 4

$\boxed{C}$

❖ Section 1 – Question 65 –

$\frac{1}{a} + \frac{1}{b} = c$ subtract $\frac{1}{b}$ from both sides

$\frac{1}{a} = c - \frac{1}{b}$ Make b the common denominator on the right side

$\frac{1}{a} = \frac{cb}{b} - \frac{1}{b}$

$\frac{1}{a} = \frac{cb - 1}{b}$ Cross multiply

b = (cb – 1) a   or $a = \frac{b}{bc - 1}$ [divide by (cb-1) on both sides]

$\boxed{C}$

SOLUTIONS

Section 2- Relations, Functions and Arithmetic sequence

- **Section 2 – Question 2** - Domain is the set of all x values and range is the set of all y values. They will be arranged from the least value to the greatest. The x values are 3, 6, 0 & -7, hence the domain D is {-7, 0, 3, 6} the y values are 7, 13, 0 and -13 so the range R is {-13, 0, 7, 13}

  $\boxed{B}$

- **Section 2 – Question 3** - A relation becomes a function when there is a single output for any unique input, so we are looking for a set of values where x is not repeating.

  $\boxed{B}$

- **Section 2 – Question 9** - Cost of 1 pound of sugar is $0.59, so the cost of P pounds of sugar is 059 × P

  C (P) = 0.59P

  $\boxed{D}$

- **Section 2 – Question 11** - To find equation from the given table, we have to find the slope first. Use any two sets of co-ordinates like (2, 8) and (3, 13). Slope m = $\frac{y_2-y_1}{x_2-x_1} = \frac{13-8}{3-2} = 5$

  Use this slope and any set of co-ordinates to find the y intercept. y= 5 x + b

  $\quad\quad\quad\quad\quad\quad\quad\quad\quad$ 8 = 5 x 2 + b [we used (2, 8)]

  $\quad\quad\quad\quad\quad\quad\quad\quad\quad$ b = -2.

  The equation of the line is y = 5 x – 2

  $\boxed{A}$

- **Section 2 – Question 13** - Given in question, f(x) = 24 – 2x and if we have to find f(2), we substitute 2 in the place of x

  $\quad\quad$ f (2) = 24 – 2 (2) = 20.

  It is given that f(x) = 10. So, we replace f(x) by 10 and solve for 'x'. This gives 10 = 24 – 2x or 2x = 14; x = 7

  The answer is 20; 7

  $\boxed{C}$

- **Section 2 – Question 17** - For any graph to be a function there should be only one output (y) corresponding to one input (x). If we look at the first graph A, the domain(x) value of x=1 have two different output (y) values of 0 and 2. Similarly x=-1 also has two different y values of 0 and -2. Same is the case with graph C for one value of x, there are two different 'y' values. Graph B has a different output(y) value for every given domain(x) value, So Graph B is a function.

  $\boxed{B}$

SOLUTIONS

- ❖ **Section 2 – Question 18** - The start of the function has a domain value starting at x = 1 and ending at x = 6. So, the domain is 1 ≤ x ≤ 6.

  The minimum value for range is 1 and the maximum value is 7. So, we can write range as 1 ≤ y ≤ 7

  $\boxed{B}$

- ❖ **Section 2 – Question 21** - The equation for the graph is given as x + 2y = -2, rearranging this equation we get 2y = -x − 2 or y = $\frac{-x}{2} - \frac{2}{2}$. Now we have to substitute the domain values one by one in this equation,

  $y = \frac{-x}{2} - 1$ Substitute $x = -4$

  $y = \frac{4}{2} - 1 = 1$ The pair is (-4, 1)

  Continue this and substitute different x values to find the corresponding y values. We get (-2, 0), (0, -1), etc. which matches with B

  $\boxed{B}$

- ❖ **Section 2 – Question 39** - The expression to find the sequence is given by 6n + 7. To get the first term, we substitute 1 in the expression

  1st term   =   6n + 7 = 6(1) + 7 = 13
  2nd term =   6n + 7 = 6(2) + 7 = 19
  3rd term   =   6n + 7 = 6(3) + 7 = 25

  $\boxed{C}$

- ❖ **Section 2 – Question 48** - The arithmetic sequence given is -9, -6, -3. We get the common difference by subtracting first term from the second term -6 - -9 = 3; d = 3

  $a_n = a_1 + (n-1)d$ where a_n is the nth term.
  We have a_n = 87, $a_1 = -9$ d = 3. Substitute the given values in a_n formula
  87 = -9 + (n - 1) 3
  96 = (n - 1)3
  32 = n – 1

  Or n = 33

  $\boxed{B}$

SOLUTIONS

Section 3- Different forms of Linear equations

- **Section 3 – Question 2** - Slope of a line is given by the formula
  $$m = \frac{y_2 - y_1}{x_2 - x_1}$$

  $3 = \frac{r-2}{7-5}$ or $3 = \frac{r-2}{2}$ Multiply by 2 on both sides

  $6 = r - 2$ Add 2 to both sides

  $r = 8$

- **Section 3 – Question 3** - Rewriting the given equation, we have $y - 3 = \frac{-2}{3}(x - 0)$. Comparing with point slope formula of line, we get line slope as $\frac{-2}{3}$, also it passes through (0, 3). Graph A has a positive slope, so it can be eliminated. The only graph that passes through (0, 3) and with the given slope is graph D.

  $\boxed{D}$

- **Section 3 – Question 8** - Any line that is the y axis or parallel to the y axis has an undefined slope. This means that they will have the same x coordinate throughout the graph. The only choice that satisfies this condition is C

  $\boxed{C}$

- **Section 3 – Question 10** - An equation to a line with a slope of $\frac{1}{2}$ and y intercept 3 can be written as $y = \frac{1}{2}x + 3$. If we have to find x intercept, we substitute the y value as zero in the equation $0 = \frac{1}{2}x + 3$ or $-3 = \frac{1}{2}x$

  $\boxed{x = -6}$

- **Section 3 – Question 16** - The line of best fit can be used to predict the total sales if we know the number of rug designs. Draw a vertical line from 110 to the line of best fit. From that point, draw a horizontal line to meet the y axis to determine total sales. The point where this horizontal line meets the y axis is the total value 35,000.

  $\boxed{D}$

- **Section 3 – Question 21** - The equation to the given line is 3x + y = 6, rearranging y = -3x+6. The slope of a line that is perpendicular to this line will be $\frac{1}{3}$ (Negative reciprocal). Equation of a line with a slope of $\frac{1}{3}$ and y intercept 2 is $y = \frac{1}{3}x + 2$.

  $\boxed{C}$

SOLUTIONS

- **Section 3 – Question 25 -** Slope of a line is given by
$$m = \frac{y_2 - y_1}{x_2 - x_1} = \frac{2k + 1 + k}{k + 1} = 5$$

    Cross multiplying, we get 3k + 1 = 5(k+1)
    Apply distributive property 3k+1 = 5k + 5
    Combine like terms -2k = 4 $\boxed{K = -2}$

- **Section 3 – Question 33 -** To find the x intercept, we have to substitute y=0 in the given equation. 0 = -9x + 75. Solving we get x = $\frac{25}{3}$. Since the x axis represents the number of DVD's, this shows that he can buy 8 DVD's.

    $\boxed{C}$

- **Section 3 – Question 50 -** First we have to find the slope of the line by using any two co-ordinates.
    (-8, -124) and (-1, -40)
$$m = \frac{-40 - -124}{-1 - -8} = \frac{84}{7} = 12$$
    All the answers are written in point slope form $y - y_1 = m(x - x_1)$ by choosing the points
    (-20, -268)
    $y + 268 = 12(x + 20)$

    $\boxed{C}$

- **Section 3 – Question 74 -** The line $y = 0$ is the x axis. Any line parallel to x axis will have a slope 0 and perpendicular to it, will have undefined slope. It should pass through (-3, -5) so it will be x = -3

    $\boxed{B}$

- **Section 3 – Question 80 -** Equation of line j is $6x + 5y = 3$
    Rearranging, we get $y = \frac{-6x}{5} + \frac{3}{5}$
    Equation of line q is 5x – 6y = 0
    Rearranging, we get $y = \frac{5}{6}x$
    The slope of line 'j' is the negative reciprocal of the slope of line q. This means they both are perpendicular to each other.

    $\boxed{D}$

SOLUTIONS

Section 4- System of Linear equations and Inequality

- **Section 4 – Question 1 –**

  $2x + 8y = 6$ Divide by 2 $\Rightarrow x + 4y = 3$

  $-5x - 20y = -15$ Divide by -5 $\Rightarrow x + 4y = 3$

  They both are the same line, which means there is infinite number of solutions.

  $\boxed{A}$

- **Section 4 – Question 6 -** Let the two numbers be x and y

  Sum of numbers = 36. So, we have x+y = 36

  Twice the first number minus the second number is 6. We can write it as 2x-y = 6

  Adding these two equations we get,

  3x = 42 or x = 14

  We know x + y = 36   14 + y = 36

  Or y = 22

  Difference of these numbers = 22 – 14 = 8

  $\boxed{B}$

- **Section 4 – Question 10 -** Let the number of small bags be represented by 'S' and the number of large bags be 'L'.

  Nora's equation for money earned is 3S + 14L = 203   (1)

  Fatima's equation for money earned is 11S + 11L = 220   (2)

  Using Elimination method here, we get

  (1) × 11 ⟶ 33S + 154 L = 2233

  (2) × -3 ⟶ -33S – 33 L = -660

  Adding both the above equations

  121 L = + 1573

  L = 13

  Now substitute value of L in the equation (2), 11S + 11 (13) = 220

  11S+143=220

  11S = 77; or S = 7

  $\boxed{D}$

- **Section 4 – Question 18 -** When the total number of songs written by drummer and guitarist is 56, we write g + d = 56

  The next equation can be written from the sentence, guitarist wrote 8 fewer songs than thrice that of drummer which is g = 3d – 8. So, the answer is A

  $\boxed{A}$

- **Section 4 – Question 21 -** The line K_1 has Y intercept as -2 and has a slope of 3. Its equation can be written as y = 3x – 2. This can be rearranged and written as 3x-y = 2 as all the answer choices are showing standard form of equation.

  The line K_2 has a Y intercept of 4 and has a slope of $\frac{-4}{9}$. The equation of the line can be written as $y = \frac{-4}{9}x + 4$. This can be rearranged as $9y = -4x + 36$

  Or 4x+9y=36

  $\boxed{A}$

SOLUTIONS

- **Section 4 – Question 29**

  $\frac{5}{14}x + \frac{2}{7}y = -1$ $\qquad\qquad$ $\frac{1}{2}x + 1y = 1$

  Multiplying by LCM of denominator

  Multiply by 14 on both sides $\qquad$ Multiply by 2 on both sides

  $5x + 4y = -14 \qquad (1)$ $\qquad\qquad$ $x + 2y = 2$

  $\qquad\qquad\qquad\qquad\qquad\qquad\qquad$ Multiply by -2 on both sides

  $\qquad\qquad\qquad\qquad\qquad\qquad\qquad$ $-2x - 4y = -4 \qquad (2)$

  Add (1) + (2) $\qquad 3x = -18 \qquad$ or $\qquad x = -6$

  Substitute $x = -6$ in (2)

  $-2(-6) - 4y = -4$

  $y = 4$ $\hfill \boxed{C}$

- **Section 4 – Question 37** - To solve a compound inequality with 'or' we find all numbers that make either of the inequalities true

  $2x - 6 < -16$ $\qquad\qquad\qquad\qquad\qquad\qquad$ $2x + 8 > 12$

  $2x < -10$ $\qquad\qquad\qquad\qquad\qquad\qquad\qquad$ $2x > 4$

  $x < -5$ $\qquad\qquad\qquad\qquad\qquad\qquad\qquad\quad$ $x > 2$

  $\hfill \boxed{A}$

- **Section 4 – Question 39** - To solve a compound inequality with 'and', we find numbers that make both inequalities true.

  $4(3x - 5) < 4(2x - 7)$ $\qquad\qquad\qquad\qquad$ $5x - 10 < 7x$

  12x-20<8x-28 $\qquad\qquad\qquad\qquad\qquad$ -10<2x

  4x-20<-28 $\qquad\qquad\qquad\qquad\qquad\qquad$ -5<x

  4x<-8

  or $x < -2$ $\qquad\qquad\qquad\qquad\qquad\qquad$ or $x > -5$

  $\hfill \boxed{B, D}$

  Combining both inequalities, $-5 < x < -2$

- **Section 4 – Question 43** - The y intercept is at 1 and the slope of the graph is -2. The portion of the graph shaded is below the line which means y is less than the inequality. We only use < sign as they have used a dotted line so $y < -2x + 1$

  $\hfill \boxed{B}$

- **Section 4 – Question 54** - The total number of quarters and dimes is 70 and can be written as D + Q = 70.

  The value of a quarter is 25 cents, and the value of a dime is 10 cents. So, the value of Q quarters is 25Q and the value of D dimes is 10D. So, the total value of the coins is 25Q + 10D. This should be equal to $9.10 or 910 cents, so the equations are Q + D = 70 and 25Q + 10D = 910

  $\hfill \boxed{D}$

SOLUTIONS

Section 5- Radicals, Exponents, and exponential functions

* **Section 5 – Question 1 -** To find missing power, apply power rule and compare the exponents, we know that $(m^5)^x = m^{-10}$, this means

    5x = -10   or   x = -2
    $2(3m^5)^x = 2(3m^5)^{-2}$
    $= 2(3^{-2} m^{-10})$
    $= \frac{2}{9} m^{-10}$

    Missing exponent = -2, coefficient = $\frac{2}{9}$ $\boxed{C}$

* **Section 5 – Question 3 -**

    $\frac{a^{15}b^{12} - a^5 b^8}{a^3 b^2}$. Let us rewrite this expression and apply quotient rule

    $\frac{a^{15}b^{12}}{a^3 b^2} - \frac{a^5 b^8}{a^3 b^2} = a^{12} b^{10} - a^2 b^6$ $\boxed{B}$

* **Section 5 – Question 4 –**

    $(4a^3 b^{-2})^{-3}$. We have to apply power rule here
    $4^{-3} (a^3)^{-3} (b^{-2})^{-3}$
    $= \frac{1}{64} a^{-9} b^6$ $=> \frac{1}{64} \frac{b^6}{a^9}$ $\boxed{A}$

* **Section 5 – Question 6 –**

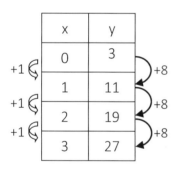

    For a linear function, rate of change (slope) should remain constant. For an exponential function, ratio of consecutive terms (y values) should remain constant.

    In this question the rate of change slope (value = 8) remains constant, hence this is linear. $\boxed{D}$

* **Section 5 – Question 9 –** $3^{1.5}$ can be written as $3^{\frac{3}{2}}$
    This means the square root of $3^3 = \sqrt{3 \times 3 \times 3} = 3\sqrt{3}$ $\boxed{B}$

* **Section 5 – Question 24 –**

    $\frac{8y^4}{4y^3} - \frac{8y^2}{4y^3} + \frac{2}{4y^3}$ We have to apply the quotient rule here, which means for an exponential division, we subtract the powers and simplify the coefficients.

    $= 2y - \frac{2}{y} + \frac{1}{2y^3}$ $\boxed{C}$

SOLUTIONS

- ❖ Section 5 – Question 35

    $r = -4 \qquad a_5 = 2 \qquad a_2 = ?$

    By explicit formula

    $a_n = a_1 r^{n-1}$

    $a_5 = a_1 r^{5-1}$

    $2 = a_1(-4)^4 \quad \text{OR} \quad 2 = 256\, a_1$

    $a_1 = \frac{2}{256} = \frac{1}{128}$

    $a_2 = a_1 r^{2-1}$

    $a_2 = \frac{1}{128}(-4) = \frac{-1}{32}$

- ❖ Section 5 – Question 39 –

    $\sqrt{20} + \sqrt{5x} + 3\sqrt{5}$ The number inside the radical sign is written as the product of a perfect square and another number, if possible

    $= \sqrt{4 \times 5} + \sqrt{5x} + 3\sqrt{5}$

    $= 2\sqrt{5} + 3\sqrt{5} + \sqrt{5x}$, combine like terms

    $= 5\sqrt{5} + \sqrt{5x}$

    [A]

- ❖ Section 5 – Question 48 - $\sqrt{27} + \sqrt{48} + \sqrt{75}$ The number inside the radical sign is written as the product of a perfect square and another number, if possible.

    $= \sqrt{9 \times 3} + \sqrt{16 \times 3} + \sqrt{25 \times 3}$

    $= 3\sqrt{3} + 4\sqrt{3} + 5\sqrt{3}$

    $= 12\sqrt{3}$

    [C]

- ❖ Section 5 – Question 56 - To find the compound interest, we have the formula

    Total Amount $= P(1 + r)^t$

    Replacing values in formula $\qquad = 100(1 + .09)^{10}$

    $= 236.74 = 236.74$

    To get the interest we have to subtract the principal amount from total amount 236.74 – 100 = 136.74. Rounding to nearest tenth, the interest is $136.70.

    [B]

- ❖ Section 5 – Question 71 -

    Half-life formula is $N = No\left(\frac{1}{2}\right)^{\frac{t}{h}}$

    No = 10

    t = 15

    h = 5

    $N = 10\left(\frac{1}{2}\right)^{\frac{15}{5}}$

    $= 10\left(\frac{1}{2}\right)^3$

    $= \frac{10}{8} = 1.25 \text{ gms}$

    [D]

SOLUTIONS

Section 6- Polynomial Functions

- **Section 6 – Question 1** - Degree of the polynomial is the highest of the degrees of each term in polynomial. For this we find the degree of each term by adding exponents of variables of each term

  $4x^3$ → Degree 3
  $-5xy^4$ → Degree = 1+4=5
  $3xy^2$ → Degree 1+2= 3

  $-5xy^4 + 4x^3 + 3xy^2 - 1$ The degree of this polynomial is 5

  $\boxed{B}$

- **Section 6 – Question 3 -**

  $4a^2 - 16a - 27a = 4a^2 - 3a + 20$ - apply distributive properly

  $4a^2 - 43a = 4a^2 - 3a + 20$ -Combine like terms.

  $-40a = 20$

  OR $a = -\dfrac{1}{2}$

  $\boxed{A}$

- **Section 6 – Question 4** - $(5t^2 - 2w)^2$

  $(5t^2 - 2w)(5t^2 - 2w)$, Rewrite the given equation

  $= 25t^4 - 20t^2w + 4w^2$, Apply distributive property

  $\boxed{D}$

- **Section 6 – Question 6** - To find the combined heights of the throws, we have to add the two polynomials. We add the like terms together

  $$\begin{array}{rrr} -11x^2 & +19x & +27 \\ -10x^2 & +10x & +18 \\ \hline -21x^2 & +29x & +45 \end{array}$$

  $\boxed{B}$

- **Section 6 – Question 9** - To find the product of two polynomials we have to multiply each term in the first polynomial with each term in the second one.

  $x^2(2x^2 + 3x + 4)$ = $2x^4 + 3x^3 + 4x^2$
  $-3x(2x^2 + 3x + 4)$ = $-6x^3 - 9x^2 - 12x$
  $6(2x^2 + 3x + 4)$ = $+12x^2 + 18x + 24$
  Adding, we get $2x^4 - 3x^3 + 7x^2 + 6x + 24$

  $\boxed{A}$

- **Section 6 – Question 24 –**

  $(x - 3)(x + 3)$ This can be solved by formula $(a - b)(a + b) = a^2 - b^2$ or using distributive property
  Using the formula
  $(x - 3)(x + 3) = x^2 - 3^2$
  $= x^2 - 9$

  $\boxed{C}$

SOLUTIONS

- **Section 6 – Question 35** - The area of a square can be found by multiplying the sides.
  Area = $(x+4)(x+4)$
  Apply distributive property
  $$= x^2 + 8x + 16$$

  [B]

- **Section 6 – Question 39** - When we factor the polynomial, we factor out the common terms first.
  $2(3-m) - 3m(m-3)$
  $= 2(3-m) - -3m(3-m)$, Factor out -ve sign to make same common factor 3-m

  $(3-m)(2+3m)$, Take out common term

  [C]

- **Section 6 – Question 54** –

  Area of a parallelogram is given by the formula A = bh   or $h = \frac{A}{b}$
  $A = 35P^6q^6$ And $b = 5Pq^2$
  $$h = \frac{35P^6q^6}{5pq^2} = 7P^5q^4$$

  [A]

- **Section 6 – Question 64** - Volume of a rectangular prism is V = l b h
  To find the depth h we do $h = \frac{v}{lb}$
  $V = 2x^3 + 9x^2 + 4x - 15$ $l = 2x + 5$ $b = x + 3$
  $lb = (2x+5)(x+3)$
  $\quad = 2x^2 + 6x + 5x + 15$ $= 2x^2 + 11x + 15$
  $h = \frac{v}{lb} = \frac{2x^3 + 9x^2 + 4x - 15}{2x^2 + 11x + 15}$

  ```
                        x - 1
                    _____
   2x² + 11x + 15 | 2x³ + 9x² + 4x - 15
                -   2x³ + 11x² + 15x
                    _____
                        -2x² - 11x - 15
                      - -2x² - 11x - 15
                        _____
                                 0
  ```

  $= x - 1$

  [A]

- **Section 6 – Question 70** - To find the revenue we have to multiply the number of games sold with the cost of 1 game Revenue = CN = $(5x+22)(9x-7)$

  [C]

SOLUTIONS

Section 7- Quadratic Functions

- **Section 7 – Question 2 –**

  $x^2 + 2x - 8 = 0$ We have to find two numbers that will give a product of -8 and sum of 2. They are +4 and -2

  $x^2 + 4x - 2x - 8 = 0$

  $x(x + 4) - 2(x + 4) = 0$ Take out the common term

  $(x + 4)(x - 2) = 0$

  Which means either $x + 4 = 0$ or $x - 2 = 0$, using zero product property

  $$x = -4 \quad \text{or } x = 2$$

  $\boxed{B}$

- **Section 7 – Question 5** - The vertex of the parabola is at (1, 0) and the graph opens upward which means 'a' is positive

  $y = a(x - h)^2 + k$

  $= 1(x - 1)^2 + 0$, simplify

  $y = x^2 - 2x + 1$

  $\boxed{A}$

- **Section 7 – Question 12** - When the value of discriminate = 0 then there will only be one real root. We can check discriminate value for each option.

  Option 1 checking whether, $b^2 - 4ac$ = 0.

  $$a = 4 \quad b = -8 \quad c = 4$$
  $$= 64 - 4(4)(4)$$
  $$= 0$$

  For the first expression itself, the discriminate is zero, so it has one real root.

  $\boxed{A}$

- **Section 7 – Question 17** - The vertex of the graph is at (1, -3) and the 'a' value is 1. so, the equation in the vertex form is

  $$y = 1(x - 1)^2 - 3$$

  $\boxed{C}$

- **Section 7 – Question 23 –**

  $x^2 - 2x - 3 = 0$ To find x intercept, we look at the points where the graph meets the x axis. It is at -1 and 3 so the co-ordinates are (-1, 0) and (3, 0). Y intercept is the point where the graph meets the y axis. It is at -3 or (0, -3)

  $\boxed{B}$

- **Section 7 – Question 26 –**

  $4x^2 + ax = 2x(2x + 1)$

  $4x^2 + ax = 4x^2 + 2x$

  This gives us: $ax = 2x$

  Or $\boldsymbol{a = 2}$

SOLUTIONS

- **Section 7 – Question 33** - Maximum point of a parabola is at the vertex. The x coordinate of vertex in standard form is given by $\frac{-b}{2a} = \frac{4}{-2} = -2$

  To find the height or y co-ordinate of vertex we substitute -2 in the equation
  $f(x) = -(-2)^2 - 4(-2) + 32$
  $= -4 + 8 + 32 = 36$

  $\boxed{C}$

- **Section 7 – Question 36 –**

  $(q + 2)^2 = 25$ Take square root on both sides
  $q + 2 = \pm 5$
  $q + 2 = 5$ Or $q + 2 = -5$
  $q = 3$ Or $q = -7$

  $\boxed{C}$

- **Section 7 – Question 40 –**

  $$3x^3 + 2x^2y + 3xy^2 + 2y^3$$

  Use grouping and factor out the common terms, we get
  $x^2(3x + 2y) + y^2(3x + 2y)$ This can also be written as $(3x + 2y)(x^2 + y^2)$

  $\boxed{A}$

- **Section 7 – Question 55** - The wider the graph, the smaller the 'a' value, so if we have to arrange graph from wider to narrower, we have to arrange the 'a' value from smaller to larger $\frac{2}{5}x^2, \frac{-4}{9}x^2, \frac{1}{2}x^2, -2x^2 - 7x^2$

  $\boxed{A}$

- **Section 7 – Question 56** - The given function is $f(x) = \frac{1}{2}x^2 + 5$, to make it narrower, it should have a higher 'a' value. Compare to given value of a=$\frac{1}{2}$. We also have to translate it 7 units down from 5, which is $5 - 7 = -2$. Both these conditions are satisfied in $g(x) = \frac{5x^2}{4} - 2$

  $\boxed{B}$

Made in United States
Orlando, FL
17 April 2025

60614790R00138